D1602842

Effective Leadership
for
Women and Men

Jerome Adams
United States Military Academy
West Point, NY

Janice D. Yoder
Webster University
St. Louis, MO

 ABLEX PUBLISHING CORPORATION
NORWOOD, NEW JERSEY

Printed in the United States of America.

Library of Congress Cataloging in Publication Data

Adams, Jerome.
  Effective leadership for women and men.

  Bibliography: p.
  Includes index.
  1. Leadership. I. Yoder, Janice. II. Title.
HM141.A33 1985   303.3′4   84-28440
ISBN 0-89391-168-2

Ablex Publishing Corporation
355 Chestnut Street
Norwood, New Jersey 07468

Contents

Preface

In May 1980 the first coeducational class was graduated from the United States Military Academy at West Point. Careful thought was given to the preparation of a volume which would rearray much of the learning about their leadership training and development. Much had been discovered and shared via sporadic papers, briefings, journal articles, and technical reports; however, we wanted to provide a complete volume suitable to academicians and to leadership practitioners.

This is not intended to be a definitive volume on women at West Point. Such a treatise is yet to be penned, no doubt, by the graduates themselves in the years to come. Rather, this book seemed to us to be especially worthwhile for persons concerned with understanding contemporary issues in leadership, what the literature prescribes, and how those engaged in management and supervision can put knowledge into practice.

Accordingly, we have organized our writing efforts into areas to promote those goals. The first two chapters unveil a theoretical framework about the dimensions of leadership: those conventionally measured factors with the addition of how gender stereotypes, sex-roles, and biological sex differences may influence the process of leadership. Quickly, the reader will note that, in theory formulation, much of what is known about leadership has been developed by men using male subjects.

In chapter 3 and 4, we describe in detail research evidence which evaluates the efficacy and the effectiveness of the various leadership theories. We emphasize those research studies which have manipulated sex-roles and sex differences of the leaders and followers to assess the utility of the theory both for women and men.

Based upon the insights gleaned from those sections we guide the reader toward a need for synthesis in chapter 5. This section offers considerations to narrow the gap between theory and practice. Chapter 6 describes how the practicing manager can use leadership in his or her organization. Although this section is, by design, the most applied, all of the other chapters contain a major portion devoted to the discussion of the implications of the knowledge both for researchers and practitioners. We conclude in chapter 7 with a perspective about future trends with specific emphasis on methodological issues and contemporary leadership practice.

This book draws upon several reports and studies about leadership which were the result of longitudinal research on the integration of women at West Point—Project Athena. The senior author directed the programs, and Jan was extensively involved in many of the studies. Thus, our knowledge comes from first-hand study and application of leadership theories in military settings. Some of the research cited involved other collaborators, and we owe a special thanks to Robert W. Rice and Deborah Instone of SUNY at Buffalo, Howard T. Prince, II, and Robert Priest at West Point, and Robert Sasmor whose basic research program funded the Athena research and Jack M. Hicks who collaborated on some of the earlier studies. Both Bob and Jack are from the Army Research Institute.

We would be remiss to overlook the important contributions of the women and men, who as cadets, were participants in many leadership studies. We were able to follow each group over an extended period of time, and that benefitted greatly our confidence in the results.

For permission to quote from their publications and to use some of the material published previously, we are grateful to the following: Fred Fiedler, Marty Chemers, McGraw Hill, and Scott Foresman Publishers; Robert R. Blake, Jane S. Mouton, and Gulf Publishing; Janet T. Spence, Robert L. Helmreich, Joy Stapp, and the University of Texas Press; Prentice Hall; and *Organizational Behavior and Human Performance Journal.*

We feel a deep debt to all of those other persons who conducted studies which we have used to help guide our thinking and writing. The citations and bibliography reflect the importance of their contributions. We also thank the staff of Ablex Publishing Corporation and unnamed others who worked closely with us in the preparation of this volume.

Finally, a special expression of gratitude is offered to my wife Debbie Adams, my sons Jerome II and Tim, and to Jan's husband John Zipp for their sustaining patience, encouragement, and support.

Jerome Adams

Jan Yoder

Chapter 1

Approaches to Understanding Leadership

Think of leaders. A wide range of people may cross your mind: politicians, bosses, presidents of corporations, committee chairpersons, team captains, and even teachers. What characteristics do these leaders share? In other words, what defines leadership? The answer to this question may seem quite simple at first. However, as we shall see in this chapter, different perspectives on leadership lead to different, often complicated answers.

WAYS TO FOCUS ON LEADERSHIP: A MATTER OF EMPHASIS

Part of the complexity of examining leadership arises from the many different ways to consider leadership. Is leadership the personal qualities that distinguish a leader from followers? If so, we are looking for distinguishing characteristics or traits of leaders. This approach necessarily leads to the next question: How did these traits come about in certain individuals and not in others? Are leaders born, not made? This question is particularly interesting when we examine sex differences in leadership.

A second way to look at leadership is to focus on the exercise of the leader's behavior. Here, we ask what leaders *do* to make themselves different from followers. While the trait approach might describe a leader as decisive, a behaviorist perspective portrays a leader as *acting* decisive by assigning tasks to group members and settling matters of members' dissatisfaction. We are now examining leadership as an activity that reflects leadership style as well as role demands.

An emphasis on how leaders emerge at the head of groups constitutes a third approach to studying leadership. Leaders may emerge from the group, be elected, or be appointed by an outside force. Each procedure for determining leadership will influence the dynamics of leadership processes within the group. Finally, we may focus on the effects of leadership on group members' performance and satisfaction. The question to answer here is: What is effective leadership?

1

Traits, leadership style, emergence, and leaders' effectiveness represent different foci from which to examine leadership. The focus shifts from spotlighting individual leaders and their traits to examining effective leaders within their social contexts. Our interest changes from the individual to a growing emphasis on group processes as we move from traits, to leadership style, to emergence, to leader effectiveness. As we will see, this shift marks the history of management thought in the study of leadership.

In this chapter, we will trace the historical development of theories of leadership dynamics from the trait approach to the situational emphasis and then to contemporary interactive theories. The latter argue that leadership is the combination of characteristics of leaders themselves and the situations (organizational and interpersonal) in which they function. Four theories will be discussed: trait, situational, contingency, and transactional. Contingency and transactional theories take an interactive perspective. More will be said about these approaches later.

CRITERIA FOR A COMPLETE THEORY

Before we explore the details of each theory, let us examine the criteria for evaluating the completeness of a theory of leadership. Although no theory is perfect, these standards will help to critically evaluate each theory by recognizing its strengths and weaknesses. Each theory (trait, situational, contingency, and transactional) is concerned with only a portion of the story about leadership. A complete theory of leadership should explain: (a) the emergence of a leader or leaders in unstructured groups; (b) the processes that maintain leader' influence over others; (c) the relation of leaders' personality (traits) and behaviors to group processes; and (d) the situations or social context in which leaders' personality and behaviors are most effective (Stogdill, 1974).

As we review each theory, keep these points in mind. Each theory will concentrate primarily on one focus and therefore will deal only with a portion of the leadership story. By realizing the strengths and gaps in each theory, we will have built a strong foundation from which to consider a more complete, and hence, more useful theory of leadership.

In the next section, we will review the four theories. Specifically, we will construct a definition of leadership that reflects each theoretical framework, briefly review the historical and theoretical background that reflects the development of each theory, and discuss the theory itself. Then, we will selectively examine some of the research spawned by each theory and the applications of real-life occurrences of leadership phenomena. Finally, we will compare and contrast the four theories with an eye to future trends.

TRAIT THEORY: PERSONAL ATTRIBUTES OF THE LEADER

Definition

According to trait theorists, leadership is determined by the personality characteristics of the person or persons who influence group members. Leadership, then, is a part of one's personality. It is reflected in personality differences between leaders and followers. The trait approach, like all personality theories, produces interesting questions about the etiology or origin of leadership traits. What causes some people to develop traits of leadership while others do not? Thus, personality theorists become caught in the nature–nurture controversy that has continued in management and in psychology as a residual of its philosophical roots (Wertheimer, 1972). Is personality, or more specifically, the traits of leadership the result of inherent (nature) or learned (nurture) capabilities?

As we shall see, trait theories are no longer accepted by contemporary scholars and practicing managers. But this question of etiology, which arose from the trait approach, is alive and well in personality theory in general and in the current literature on leadership. The recent interest in sex differences in leadership is largely responsible for this resurgence of interest in the nature–nurture debate as it relates to leadership phenomena. We will take up this question when we examine applications of this theoretical perspective.

Background

Interest in the trait approach grew from practical necessity during World War I. The U.S. Army was interested in efficiently screening and selecting persons for military service. The military leaders sought the help of the American Psychological Association. A group of eminent researchers was assembled, and they worked together to produce such noteworthy accomplishments as the Army Alpha Intelligence Test and a rating scale of officers' qualifications for service. These fulfilled a pragmatic demand for tests of leadership that could be administered easily and be scored quickly and quantitatively. This utility greatly influenced the development of the trait perspective. With the conclusion of the war, industry continued this research on screening for use in personnel recruitment (Stogdill, 1974).

Trait researchers explored a broad range of individual characteristics, focusing mostly on physique, social background, intelligence, and personality (Nutting, 1923; Stogdill, 1948, 1980). These studies concluded that leaders as compared with nonleaders tended to be taller, more physically attractive, more intelligent and self-confident, psychologically healthier, dominant, extroverted, and more sensitive to other people (Gibb, 1969). No doubt, it is with these studies in mind that the physically shorter Jimmy Carter demanded podiums and a platform for the Ford–Carter debates in the 1976 presidential election. Also, Ronald Reagan's film and media background has been a helpful experience in winning public support as a charismatic president.

Reviewers of the research conducted by trait theorists agreed that the measurement of personality factors has not proven very useful for the selection of leaders (Stogdill, 1974). However, it was not until the advent of World War II that the emphasis shifted from personality traits and paper-and-pencil testing to an interest in leadership style.

LEADERSHIP STYLE: A BEHAVIORIST VIEW

Leadership style is conceptually very similar to the trait approach and, for that reason, both will be discussed together. While trait theories focus upon the actual characteristics of leaders, theorists interested in leadership style concentrate on the ways in which leaders manifest their leadership. The focus here is on the behaviors of leaders as they influence group members, and how these behaviors are regarded as examples of leaders' style.

Definition

According to the leadership style approach, leadership is "the behavior of an individual when he [or she] is directing the activities of a group toward a shared goal" (Hemphill & Coons, 1957, p. 7). Note that the focus is still solely on leaders themselves. Followers supply a bland background from which leaders stand forward in contrast. The situation or context in which leaders play a part is ignored.

The difference between the trait and behavioral approaches is a matter of emphasis. The trait theorists stress what leaders *are* in terms of the personality characteristics or traits which they have internalized, whereas the behavior or style theorists highlight what leaders *do* when they lead.

Background

During and after World War II, the empirical climate favored the use of controlled group experiments and surveys rather than personality testing (Stogdill, 1974). Researchers explored the relationship between leaders' style and group performance and satisfaction. The search for leaders ended while the search for effective leadership styles flourished. A classic study of leadership style was conducted by Lewin, Lippit, and White (1939). Three fundamental styles of leadership were identified: autocratic, democratic, and laissez-faire. Autocratic leaders centralize power in themselves and dominate the decision-making processes of the group. Groups succeed or fail according to the effectiveness of the autocratic leaders themselves.

Leaders who exhibit a democratic style share their power and responsibilities with group members. Decisions are made by consensus or group agreement. Democratic leadership requires strong, open lines of communication so that all group members participate fully in group activities. Initially, decision making may be slow when the ideas of all group members must be solicited and discussed.

In contrast, laissez-faire leadership is akin to no leadership at all. No one formally or informally shoulders the responsibility of leadership, and the group often flounders when it is forced to make a decision.

Lewin et al. (1939) trained adult leaders of hobby clubs for 10-year-old boys to act according to each of these three leadership styles. The purpose of the experiment was to explore how these three styles related to the performance and atmosphere of each group. In order to avoid confusing leadership style with the personality characteristics that each adult naturally brought to the task, the researchers rotated the adult leaders every 6 weeks with different groups of boys and with each leadership style. Here we see an illustration of controlled experimentation. In this way, every leader was autocratic, democratic, or laissez-faire at some time during the experiment. Members of the hobby clubs had two goals: to complete specified tasks and to have fun.

Autocratic leaders determined all policy, directed activities, and assigned tasks and partners. They remained aloof from the boys. When children worked under an autocratic leader, they spent a great deal of time working on specified tasks and met only their task goals. When the leader left the room, tasks were quickly forgotten and were resumed only under the close supervision of the leader. Hostile outbursts were more frequent in this group than the other groups, resulting in overt aggression and destruction of property.

On the other hand, leaders trained to be democratic suggested alternative approaches to a decision but left the decision making itself to group members. Members were free to select their own tasks and work companions. These leaders participated in group affairs. Group cohesiveness was highest under democratic leadership and both task and group goals were achieved. Although democratically run groups spent more time performing their tasks than did children under autocratic leadership, their products were of higher quality and reflected greater originality and creativity. They continued to work in the absence of the leader.

Laissez-faire leaders barely participated in group activities. At most, adults playing this role would supply information when asked. The amount and quality of work accomplished under this type of leadership was poor, and although participants felt that they had accomplished their social goals, they showed little evidence of completing task goals.

The work of Lewin and his colleagues has been replicated both in the field (Morse & Riemer, 1956) and the laboratory (Preston & Heintz, 1949; Shaw, 1955). A combination of high group productivity and satisfaction is found under conditions of democratic leadership. Yet, this simple statement and the ones made by the trait theorists are not consistently true. For example, Scott (1952) found that in the military, morale often is highest under autocratic leadership. It is this situational specificity that plagues trait and style theories with their focus on leaders. We will return to this point when we evaluate trait theories. Now, let us look at other examples of research on leadership style.

Theory

Lewin, Lippit, and White (1939) gave the leadership-style perspective two types of leaders: autocratic and democratic. (Remember that laissez-faire leaders are actually not leaders at all, because they fail to influence the group.) *Autocratic* or authoritative leaders seek to impose their own will on the group and thereby dominate it, whereas *democratic* leaders regard themselves as instruments of the group to be used to further the welfare of the group. To this list, later researchers added four more leadership styles (Stogdill, 1974): (a) *persuasive* leaders appeal to the sentiments of followers, whereas (b) *representative* leaders act as spokespersons for the group as a whole; (c) leaders who demonstrate strong administrative skills within formally structured organizations are called *executive* leaders; and (d) *intellectual* leaders rely on their prominence or expertise in a given field.

Think of leaders you know for each of these six categories. How do they maintain their influence as leaders? In each case, leaders become and remain leaders through their exercise of power. It is not surprising that Raven and Kruglanski (1970) described six types of personal power that form the basis of each type of leadership.

Coercive and reward power arise from the leader's ability to punish and reward the activities of followers (Raven & French, 1958). Autocratic leaders rely on this source of power as the foundation of their influence. Autocratic leaders will remain powerful and in a position of leadership as long as they control resources desired by group members. In other words, followers will allow the autocratic leader to influence them as long as the leader controls rewards that followers seek within the group or as long as the leader can influence followers' compliance via threat or punishment.

Democratic leaders use reciprocal influence to cement their leadership. Reciprocal power is built upon an exchange relationship: In exchange for the power of leadership, the democratic leader takes the responsibility of protecting and enhancing the welfare of the group. We will have more to say about this process in chapter 2.

Persuasive leadership is based on informational power. Here, leaders persuasively communicate with their followers to convince them of the rationality or benefits of a specific course of action. The extent to which leaders can convince followers is indicative of the amount of informational power they can exercise. Physicians, football coaches, and college professors are all examples of leaders with informational power.

Referent power is derived from people's ability to influence others who identify with them. In other words, when Bruce Jenner advertises Wheaties, he is trying to influence viewers' behavior to buy this brand of cereal and become as strong as Jenner. We tend to identify with people who are attractive, powerful, and competent (Bandura, 1962) or similar to ourselves in background and values (Raven & Kruglanski, 1970). Representative leaders with whom members of the group identify are able to present themselves as spokespersons for the group as a whole.

Executive leaders are strong administrators filling a designated position such as a chief executive officer, within a formally structured organization. Some of their influence arises from the position they hold. Influence derives from the authority invested in the position itself; this is called legitimate power.

Finally, intellectual leaders draw upon their expert power to exercise their leadership. Expert power arises from a reputation for being knowledgable. This reputation may be supported by formal credentials (such as a doctoral degree), experience, or the success or failure of past predictions and decisions (Hollander & Julian, 1969).

Each leadership style is related to at least one form of personal power. Actual leaders may use several different styles and hence different sources of power to attain and maintain their position. Different styles may be appropriate at different phases of leadership. For example, a leader may rise to power using coercive and reward power, but maintain his or her position with a more democratic style. Again, we are touching on the interrelation of style with situational variables—a discussion we will postpone.

The important point here is that theories of leadership style, because they focus on leaders themselves, stress the power or influence of leaders. As we defined earlier, leadership indeed is an influence process. The type of influence described here is unilateral—flowing downward from powerful leaders to followers. Even reciprocal power is examined to the extent to which it enhances leaders' power, and not that of followers'.

Research Findings

An abundance of research on leadership style was generated by the development of the Leader Opinion Questionnaire (LOQ) and the Leader Behavior Description Questionnaire (LBDQ) as part of the Ohio State Leadership Studies (Hemphill & Coons, 1957; Shartle, 1950). Starting with a large number of questionnaire items thought to be descriptive of leaders, these researchers found that two general qualities describe leadership style: consideration and initiation of structure.

Consideration includes exhibitions by the leader of concern for the welfare of followers. Considerate supervisors showed appreciation for good work, treated subordinates as equals, emphasized job satisfaction, worked hard to make others feel at ease, were easy to approach, solicited and acted upon suggestions, and discussed decisions before making them. Inconsiderate leaders publicly criticized others, did not consider others' feelings, and refused to accept suggestions and explain decisions (Bass, 1981).

Leaders initiated structure to the extent that they originated group activities, organized them, and defined the procedures for accomplishing tasks. Leaders high in initiation of structure clearly defined their own and others' work tasks in the group, outlined standards of performance, set deadlines, and decided in detail what should be done and how to do it.

Leaders given the Leaders Opinion Questionnaire were scored as being either high or low on both initiation of structure and consideration. Although any combination is possible, most studies showed that leaders who scored high in consideration were likely to also receive high scores for initiation of structure (Schriesheim, House, & Kerr, 1976).

Studies relating leaders' LBDQ scores and followers' satisfaction and performance furnished mixed results. Employees' perceptions of how considerate their supervisor was were positively related to group productivity (Lawshe & Nagle, 1953) and unit effectiveness (Besco & Lawshe, 1959). Medium and high degrees of consideration, in combination with low degrees of initiation of structure, were associated with the lowest rates of employee turnover and grievance (Fleishman & Harris, 1962). In the military, Air Force crew members' satisfaction was positively related to consideration and negatively correlated with initiation of structure during training, whereas the relationship between satisfaction and both styles of leadership was positive for the same crew members during combat (Halpin, 1954).

The conclusion is the one we have heard previously: leader style does not exist in isolation. Rather, leadership style interacts with the situation and the followers that make up the complete group picture. Generally, supervisory consideration is associated with subordinates' satisfaction with their supervisor, few absences, and low turnover. Leaders' willingness to initiate structure is considered either positive or negative, depending upon the type of personnel involved, the work environment, and the goals and constraints of the situation (Bass, 1981).

Application

How many politicians are women? Think of the members of the two houses of Congress. In 1982 (the 97th Congress), only 19 of the 435 Representatives in the House and 2 of 100 Senators were women ("Women increase," 1980).[1] In the business world, only 4.8% of all working women in 1975 were managers, officials, and proprietors (*Handbook of Labor Statistics,* 1975, p. 41), and 26% of all managers in 1980 were women (U.S. Bureau of the Census, 1981). In academia in 1978, women represented only 10% of all full professors, while they filled 28% of the lowest level positions as assistant professors (Allen, 1979, p. 10). Clearly, women are underrepresented as leaders.

Trait and style theories, with their focus on individual leaders, encourage us to ask why women fail to be in leadership roles. Do women not possess the necessary traits, such as assertiveness, task orientation, achievement motivation, or style to be leaders?

In her well-publicized studies, Horner (1970, 1972) discovered that women often derogated successful women. When subjects were asked to describe Anne, who was at the top of her medical school class, they wrote degrading stories about her. She was depicted as a pimply faced loner and a woman torn by conflicts between career and familial success. These stories lead Horner, with her person-centered perspective, to postulate that women were motivated (or, more precisely, demotivated) by fear of success. She argued that this deficiency of women is responsible for their failure to attain positions of leadership.

Liberal researchers set out to uncover the etiology of this presumed lack of achievement motivation in women. They discovered that the parents of most boys and of girls who grew up to pursue successful careers were interested and involved in the achievement activities of their children (Angrist & Almquist, 1975; Birnbaum, 1975; Ginzberg, 1966). Furthermore, the ratio of female to male underachievers increases with age. As children grow older, fewer and fewer boys remain as underachievers, whereas the number of girls who fail to realize their potential increases (Raph, Goldberg, & Passow, 1966; Shaw & McCuen, 1960). Clearly, fear of success is learned.

Still, this leaves us with a picture of contemporary women who are incapable of successfully filling the position of a leader. Additional research changes this picture. Monahan, Kuhn, and Shaver (1974) asked both men and women to write a story about Anne. Men as well as women belittled Anne's accomplishments. On the other hand, both men and women wrote favorably about John, who also scored at the top of his medical school class. Do women fear success, or do both men and women fear successful women?

Cherry and Deaux (in Deaux, 1976a, pp. 52–53) asked both women and men to describe Anne and John who were at the top of either their medical-school or nursing-school class. Negative stories were composed only about Anne as a competent physician and John as a competent nurse. The key then is the out-of-role nature of their successes. When success in a given field is inappropriate according to our sex-role stereotypes, we will degrade people

---

[1]These levels are the highest ever achieved in both legislative bodies.

who strive for and attain success in these sex-role inappropriate areas. Thus, it is not success itself which women and men fear; rather, it is success at inappropriate tasks. Focusing solely on individuals as leaders again proves to be inadequate. The situation in which leadership takes place also is important and cannot be ignored.

Evaluation

Given the four standards for judging the completeness of a theory of leadership, the theories of leaders' traits and style indeed are incomplete. With Lewin, Lippit, and White's (1939) classic study and the multitude of studies spawned by the Ohio State Leadership Studies and the LBDQ, the theory of leadership style has been most effective in relating leaders' styles to group processes, such as satisfaction and performance. It is this contribution to the early portion of a comprehensive view of leadership that continues to make a review of the style approach important.

The theories of traits and leadership style do not address the questions of how leaders emerge and maintain their postitions. These approaches also ignore the interaction of leaders with followers (Bass, 1981) and hence fail to contribute in these areas. Both perspectives envision a one-way flow of power from leaders to followers.

The most telling criticism against trait theories focuses upon their inability to delineate the situations or social context in which a given trait, style, or combination of these produces the most effective leadership pattern (Bass, 1981). Time and time again findings were being qualified to fit only certain types of followers working within a specific social context. Because of the situational specificity of trait theories, they are no longer regarded alone but rather have been incorporated into other, more complicated theories such as contingency theory.

Also, there are three methodological difficulties with trait theories. First, traits or styles do not operate in isolation. Each trait is only one element within the complex personality profile of each and every individual (Stodgill, 1974). To pinpoint only one trait and relate it to leadership fails to take into account the remaining unique combination of personality components that also are actively influencing the leadership dynamics observed by the researcher.

Second, most research on traits and style is correlational; that is, these associative studies do not explain causal relationships. This leaves unanswered many questions about the etiology of these traits. We often assume that because a leader possesses certain traits or a particular style, he or she rises to power and maintains that position. However, it is just as possible for those traits to develop in the leader in response to situational demands once he or she aspires to and attains that position. The direction of causality is unclear (Kleinhans & Taylor, 1976).

Finally, in most studies the same person rated both leadership and traits or style. It is possible that the raters' expectations about what defines good leadership influenced their scoring (Kleinhans & Taylor, 1976). For example, if a rater believed that good leaders should be intelligent and he or she considered person X to be a good leader, the rater may describe person X as intelligent, regardless of that person's actual capabilities.

Although trait and style theories are no longer examined as complete theoretical perspectives, the findings discussed here have been incorporated into recent interactive theories. Before we examine these current theories, let us take a brief look at the situational theories.

SITUATION THEORY: LEADERSHIP AS A ROLE

Definition

According to the situation approach, *leadership is a role* (Sherif & Sherif, 1956). Roles are expectations about how all people in a given position should think or act (Hollander, 1981). Roles do not exist within individuals as traits do; rather, roles arise from the social context in which they take place. The leadership role is not static but changes with the situation. Thus, leadership may differ among groups and within a specific group over time. It is upon these differences in groups and the situations that they created that we now focus.

Background

With the failure of trait and style theories to explain the emergence and maintenance of leadership, researchers began focusing on the situation to gain insights into these portions of the leadership picture. Bales and Slater (1955) observed two types of leader roles that emerge in certain groups: instrumental and socioemotional, or expressive. The instrumental role concentrates on task elements of the group, whereas the socioemotional role deals with members' satisfaction, morale, and group atmosphere. Sometimes one leader plays both roles; however, these roles frequently are filled by different persons. Note that these positions are not created by qualities that a leader brings to the group; rather, they are developed by the group itself as necessary functions to be orchestrated by suitable individuals.

Furthermore, groups are dynamic. The roles they create and foster evolve with the development of the group. In reviewing some 60 studies, Tuckman (1965) suggested that groups evolve through four stages:

1. *informing:* characterized by testing of potential leaders and elimination of others;

2. *storming:* characterized by a struggle for leadership among remaining contenders;
3. *norming:* marked by developing group cohesiveness and expectations; and
4. *performing:* designated by effective task performance and interrelationships among group members.

The leaders' role changes through these stages from effective campaigner to team leader to instrumental decision maker and socioemotional caretaker.

Theory

Situation theory focuses on the characteristics of the task and situation or social context in which leadership is enacted. Leadership patterns varied according to the amount of structure inherent in the group's tasks (e.g., Fiedler, 1964), the clarity of task objectives (Farrow, Valenzi, & Bass, 1980), the routineness of procedures (Walker & Guest, 1952), task complexity (Bell, 1967), and task difficulty (Morris, 1966). Even the type of task, intellectual versus manual, makes a difference in who emerges as leader (Carter, Haythorn, & Howell, 1950).

The task itself may influence the style with which leaders do their jobs. After 20 Naval officers had been transferred, researchers examined both the former and new officers (Stogdill, Shartle, Scott, Coons, & Jaynes, 1956). After several months in their new positions, transferred officers resembled their predecessors in their patterns of work behavior but not in patterns of interpersonal behavior. The task requirements of the job subtly influenced the work behaviors of whomever filled that job.

The situation within which leadership takes place can be divided into three aspects: interpersonal, organizational, and societal. The interpersonal component is reflected in thinking of leadership as a role. Remember that roles are expectations about how people should think and act in a given position (Hollander, 1981). When we think of leadership as a role, we consider the expectations we hold for leaders. For example, we expect leaders to be male, self-reliant, aggressive, helpful, and competent (Schein, 1973). Roles do not exist in isolation. Roles are interpersonal and complementary. For every leader role, there is a follower role, for every supervisor, a worker. Thus, roles reflect the interpersonal nature of leadership.

Leadership also occurs within a given organization and is, in turn, shaped by the characteristics of that organization. For example, the type of leadership exercised is contingent upon the formality of the organization (Hare, 1957), whether it is flat or hierarchical (Carzo & Yanouzas, 1969), centralized with one head or decentralized (Kline & Martin, 1958), and structurally complex or simple (Bryson & Kelley, 1978).

Finally, leadership is practiced within specific societal or cultural contexts and hence is influenced by norms. Norms, in contrast with roles, are expectations about how *all* people should think and act in *all* positions (Hollander, 1981). While nurturance may be part of the parenting role, helping others who have helped you is a general societal rule reflecting the norm of reciprocity (Gouldner, 1960). In leadership, the emphasis on competition and achievement (McClelland, 1961) that marks a capitalist society produces a much different picture of leadership than would arise in a different society. Societal patterns necessarily influence the nature of leadership.

Research Findings

Does the mayor direct the city (trait approach) or does the city direct the mayor (situational approach)? This is the basic research question Salanick and Pfeffer (1977) attempted to answer in their analysis of 30 U.S. cities between 1951 and 1968.

One of the primary charges of a city's mayor is to determine budgetary policy, that is, to take in tax revenues and decide upon expenditures for police, fire, highways, hospitals, parks, and libraries. Salanick and Pfeffer (1977) set out to assess (a) how much of budgetary allocations were determined by mayors, characteristics of the cities, and the historical period, and (b) if vocal public interest groups restricted mayoral discretion on issues important to the farmer.

The impact of the mayor was measured by noting changes in budgetary allotments coinciding with the election of a different mayor. The impact of the city included its size, its economic base, the characteristics of its population, the political context, and the administrative procedures followed by municipal officals. The effects of the historical period included those elements of national policy which impinge on municipal operation, such as the general unemployment rate, the state of the economy, and federal environmental policies.

Salanick and Pfeffer (1977) found that the characteristics of cities were significantly more influential on budgetary decisions than the mayors who held office. Whereas mayors accounted for only between 5% and 15% of the variance in budgetary allocations, the cities greatly affected these decisions, accounting for between 70% and 90% of the variance. Although mayors play some part in influencing budgetary distributions, their role is dwarfed by the cities themselves.

Furthermore, budgetary decisions concerning a large segment of a mayor's constituency (e.g., police and fire) were influenced less by the mayors than were those expenditures important to only a few special interest groups (e.g., parks and libraries). The mayors contributed less than 7% to the former areas; over 15% to the latter. The limited discretion of mayors is curtailed even more in those areas in which they are accountable to large segments of their constituency.

This does not mean that mayors play no role in municipal governance. They do. However, these findings highlight the situational constraints within which mayors and other leaders must work. Furthermore, the impact of situational influences is not restricted to local government. Similar findings were reported in manufacturing industries (Lieberson & O'Connor, 1972). Our tendency to blame the leader and call for a change, such as the musical chairs played by some baseball managers (Gamson & Scotch, 1964), reflects our apparent overemphasis on trait over situation approaches.

Application

A situational approach to sex-role and biological sex differences in leadership is emerging in contemporary social psychology (see Hollander & Yoder, 1980).[2] Much research concentrated on the interpersonal and organizational influences on leadership for women and men. Research on leadership in general, and particularly on women as leaders, needs to be done with a societal perspective in order to complete the situationally oriented picture.

The leader role is a masculine one. People generally expect the leader to be a man (Inderlied & Powell, 1979), and when research subjects choose the future leader of a group, men were more likely than women to select themselves (Eskilson & Wiley, 1976). In business, when respondents were asked to give three separate ratings of successful middle managers, Schein (1973) found that the ratings for men and middle managers overlapped for 60 of 86 items. In contrast, evaluations of women in general showed them to be similar to successful middle managers on only 8 of the 86 items. The roles of manager and women were incongruent. Furthermore, a more recent replication of this study revealed that this pattern persists (Massengill & DiMarco, 1979).

The sex-role stereotyping of the leader role is so pervasive as to negate the influence of leaders' personality characteristics. In a revealing study by Megargee (1969), a particular personality trait called dominance was paired with the sex of participants. According to personality theories, the dominant partner should arise as leader, and this is exactly what happened when dominant men were paired with submissive women. When the partners scored similarly on dominance (either both high or both low), the male took over in

---

[2]The reader should note that in contemporary literature, especially in the *Journal of Sex-Roles* and *The Psychology of Women Quarterly*, the terms *sex roles* and *gender* are used interchangeably. The term to denote difference between men and women is *biological sex differences*. We will adapt this convention in terminology. Thus, *sex differences* referes to physiological differences, and *gender* refers to psychological or culturally stereotyped sex-roles ascribed to men and women (Unger, 1974).

accordance with the sex-typing of the leader role. In the most interesting condition, when a dominant woman was matched with a submissive man, *she* decided that *he* should be the leader. The sex-typing of the role exerted a greater influence on the outcome (although not on the process) of this appointment than personality style did. Clearly, perceptions about the leadership role are potent variables in determining leadership.

The importance of organizational factors in affecting leadership in the corporate world is highlighted by Rosabeth Moss Kanter (1977). She argues that differences in opportunity, power, and numbers as features of the organization limit women's accession to managerial positions. Through her intensive observations and analyses of a large corporation, Kanter proposed that the system of promotion, which showed that few women were, in actuality, advancing up the corporate ladder, stifled the commitment and aspirations of most women and a few men. Those people who saw little opportunity were, in turn, not promoted because of their apparent lack of commitment and career aspirations. The vicious cycle becomes self-propogating—a continual self-fulfilling prophecy (Merton, 1968). A similar scenario can be constructed regarding power.

The importance of numbers is another story. *Tokens* are defined as members of a subgroup who compose less than 15% of the entire group (Kanter, 1977). Tokens are those who were admitted to the larger group through pressure from external sources, and who remain marginal and not fully accepted by their peers (Laws, 1975). Women in managerial positions frequently fit this definition.

Kanter (1977) continues to show that as tokens, women are exposed to excessive performance pressures because of their visibility. Picture a corporate board room. The corporate officers sit around a mahogany table. One is a woman; the remainder are men. Who stands out? Consider what this does to the young, ambitious male executive sitting to her right. He wants to be in the spotlight (when he succeeds), but he must wrestle it away from her. He envies her "competitive edge," never considering that the spotlight is constant for her, even when she fails. Also, think about the other board members. How do they react to this female intruder? Can they tell the same stories they told previously? Or go to the same club after work? They are uncertain about her.

Finally, how do the members of the dominant group ease their uncertainties about the token? They encapsulate her into a role—the role of a woman. Remember that this feminine role is incompatible with the managerial role. Our managerial woman finally represents all women, gives the "women's" point of view and grapples with role ambiguity and conflict for herself. Certainly this is not the kind of organizational atmosphere that is conducive to redefining the leadership role to include women.

What can be done? Discriminatory hiring and promotional practices can be legally abolished. Opportunities and the power that comes with them then will materialize. The numbers of women in leadership positions will increase, abolishing the side effects of tokenism. Even attitudes may change as women as leaders become commonplace, and competition with men (as well as other women) is less keen (Yoder, Adams, Grove, & Priest, 1983). Although these may seem like dreams, research on similar processes to change racial discrimination and prejudice is encouraging. Researchers continue to show that change is possible (Aronson, Blaney, Sikes, Stephen, & Snapp, 1975; Cook, 1971; Deutsch & Collins, 1951; Ramirez, 1977).

Evaluation

The situation theory arose primarily as a reaction to the trait theories that dominated the research on leadership processes. As a reaction, this theory demonstrated the importance of situational variables in predicting the emergence of leaders and understanding their continuation in that role as it evolves over time. The theory complements the ability of trait theories to relate leaders' personality to group processes. It will take a combination of these two approaches to cover the three aspects of leadership theory as well as to contribute to the fourth criterion which seeks to understand leaders' effectiveness by knowing both situational and personality characteristics.

The remaining two theories, contingency and transactional, are interactive. They posit that leadership is a combination of personality and situational factors. Each theory specifies different aspects of personality and the situation and, as Stogdill (1974) argues, each is incomplete. Yet, each has progressed in whittling down a vague, apparently reasonable assumption (that situation and personality interact) to a manageable size that is conducive for generating and testing hypotheses as well as advising practitioners.

CONTINGENCY THEORY: A BLEND OF LEADER STYLE WITH THE SITUATION

Definition

Effective leadership results from the right combination of situational favorability and leadership style. The key to effective leadership is the degree to which leaders' style and the properties of the situation are well matched. Leadership style is regarded as a trait—something leaders bring with them to the situation. Style is not regarded as a quality of leaders that is molded by the situation, as situational theorists argue. Rather, style is a predisposition that is either appropriate or inappropriate within given situational contingencies. Hence, effective leadership is contingent upon the degree to which leaders' style and situational factors match.

Background

As we have seen, both trait and situational theories were not comprehensive theories of leadership. Yet, each approach seems to offer the student of leadership some insights into this elusive phenomenon. Furthermore, based on Stodgill's (1974) criteria for evaluating each theory, both perspectives are most deficient in understanding effective leadership. With renewed interest in the application of leadership research to personnel selection and training came an emphasis on leaders' effectiveness. On a superficial level, the path of future research on leadership was clear: Explore the effectiveness of leadership by combining the trait and situational approaches. One attempt to do this in detail was offered by Fiedler's (1964, 1967) contingency model.

The antecedent conditions for contingency theory arose from the situational and style literature. By pointing to the interpersonal and organizational influences on leadership, situational theory provided the general direction for Fiedler's theory. It is within this vague orientation that Fiedler needed to specify clearly the characteristics of the interpersonal and organizational situation most impactful to effective leadership.

The literature on leaders' style offered a less ambiguous road map. The Leader Behavior Description Questionnaire (LBDQ) exposed two patterns of leaders' behavior: consideration and initiation of structure. The assumption of the LBDQ is that these behaviors reflected the leadership style of actual leaders. However, as we have seen in the previous section, it is possible that these behaviors were the consequence of situational pressures to exhibit them.

Paralleling these two types of leader behavior are two styles: task-oriented (initiation of structure:autocratic) and relations-oriented (consideration:democratic). Task-oriented leaders are concerned primarily with reaching the goals set by the group. Research of task-oriented leaders showed a personality style that is aloof from group members (Blau & Scott, 1962), work-facilitative and goal emphasizing (Bowers & Seashore, 1966), aggressive-competitive, resourceful, and self-sufficient (Bass & Dunteman, 1963).

Relations-oriented leaders take a human relations approach concentrating on affable, warm interpersonal relationships with and among followers. This leader style shows strong concern for people (Blake & Mouton, 1964), is sociable, and includes needs for affiliation (Bass & Dunteman, 1963). It is upon these two well-researched leadership styles that Fiedler built his contingency theory.

Theory

LPC. Contingency theory combines leaders' style and situational favorability to predict leaders' effectiveness. Leaders' style is measured by

EFFECTIVE LEADERSHIP FOR WOMEN AND MEN

Table 1
The Least Preferred Co-worker Scale

Think of the person with whom you can work *least well*. This person may be someone you work with now or someone you knew in the past. This person does not have to be the person you like least well, but should be the person with whom you had the most difficulty in getting a job done.

Please describe this person as he or she appears to you by putting an "X" in the appropriate space on the following scales.

Pleasant :___:___:___:___:___:___:___:	Unpleasant
Friendly :___:___:___:___:___:___:___:	Unfriendly
Rejecting :___:___:___:___:___:___:___:	Accepting
Helpful :___:___:___:___:___:___:___:	Frustrating
Unenthusiastic :___:___:___:___:___:___:___:	Enthusiastic
Tense :___:___:___:___:___:___:___:	Relaxed
Distant :___:___:___:___:___:___:___:	Close
Cold :___:___:___:___:___:___:___:	Warm
Cooperative :___:___:___:___:___:___:___:	Uncooperative
Supportive :___:___:___:___:___:___:___:	Hostile
Boring :___:___:___:___:___:___:___:	Interesting
Quarrelsome :___:___:___:___:___:___:___:	Harmonious
Self-Assured :___:___:___:___:___:___:___:	Hesitant
Efficient :___:___:___:___:___:___:___:	Inefficient
Gloomy :___:___:___:___:___:___:___:	Cheerful
Open :___:___:___:___:___:___:___:	Guarded

From *Theory of Leader Effectiveness* (p. 41) by F. E. Fiedler, 1967, New York: McGraw Hill. Copyright 1967 by McGraw-Hill Publishers. Reprinted by permission.

their score on the LPC (Least Preferred Co-worker) scale. Respondents are asked to describe an actual person or type of person with whom they worked least well. Before reading further, you may want to complete the LPC scale in Table 1 and calculate your score.

To score the LPC scale, score the favorable pole of each item (pleasant, friendly, accepting, etc.) as 8 and the unfavorable pole as 1. Note some of the items are reversed (e.g., friendly, then rejecting). Still, the favorable item "friendly" is scored as 8. The unfavorable item "rejecting" is scored as 1. The intermediate spaces should be scored from 2 to 7 in accordance with the end points. The sum of these 8-point ratings is your LPC score (Fiedler, Chemers, & Mahar, 1976). A high LPC score is approximately 82 and above; low LPC, 81 and below.

If your score on the LPC scale is high, you are classified as a relations-oriented person; low, a task-oriented leader. Your score on this scale is relatively stable, that is, you will consistently score as either a high or low LPC (Rice, 1978a). Furthermore, in a comprehensive review of possible interpretations of what this LPC score measures, the evidence supports the conclusion that LPC scores reflect the degree of task and relations orientation of respondents (Rice, 1978b).

A closer examination of the LPC scale makes this interpretation clearer. To receive a low score, a respondent may describe his or her least preferred co-worker as someone with whom he or she cannot work (incompetent; inefficient) and dislikes interpersonally (unpleasant; cold). On the other hand, a high-LPC, relations-oriented person may not like working with this least preferred co-worker and hence also describe him or her in negative, task-related terms, although this respondent still may feel liking or concern for this co-worker as reflected by higher ratings on interpersonal items (e.g., friendly and interesting). In other words, task-oriented leaders, concerned with getting the job done, do not like the people with whom they cannot work, and hence rate their least preferred co-worker negatively on all items of the LPC scale. This produces a low overall score. In contrast, relations-oriented leaders, concerned with people, may be able to like those with whom they cannot work. These high interpersonal ratings will result in a higher overall score for relations-oriented leaders.

Situational favorability. Three factors determine situational favorability: leader–member relations, task structure, and position power. Leader–member relations, one component of the interpersonal aspect of the situation, is the most important factor. Leaders having positive interpersonal relationships with members are in favorable circumstances. These positive relations include both liking and respect.

Task structure and position power are organizational factors. A task is clearly structured if the goals of the task are known, if there is only one viable solution to the task, and if a decision can be verified by objective feedback. A task is less structured to the extent that these three task characteristics are not met. As the degree of structure declines, the more problematic is the task for the leader.

Table 2
Group Atmosphere Scale

Describe the atmosphere of your group by checking the following items.

Friendly :___:___:___:___:___:___:___:	Unfriendly
Accepting :___:___:___:___:___:___:___:	Rejecting
Satisfying :___:___:___:___:___:___:___:	Frustrating
Enthusiastic :___:___:___:___:___:___:___:	Unenthusiastic
Productive :___:___:___:___:___:___:___:	Nonproductive
Warm :___:___:___:___:___:___:___:	Cold
Cooperative :___:___:___:___:___:___:___:	Uncooperative
Supportive :___:___:___:___:___:___:___:	Hostile
Interesting :___:___:___:___:___:___:___:	Boring
Successful :___:___:___:___:___:___:___:	Unsuccessful

From *Theory of Leader Effectiveness* (p. 267) by F. E. Fiedler, 1967, New York: McGraw Hill. Copyright 1967 by McGraw-Hill publishers. Reprinted by permission.

Before reading further, you may with to classify the task structure of your work group, using Table 2 to calculate your score.

To score the group atmosphere scale, follow the procedure set forth earlier for the LPC scale. That is, the favorable pole will be awarded an 8 and an unfavorable pole a 1. The other points along the continuum remain from 2 to 7 in accordance with the end points. Sum the score of the items.

The final organizational factor to consider in situational favorability is position power or the legitimate authority of the leader. Position power refers to the degree of legitimate authority inherent in the position of leadership itself. The more legitimate, coercive, and reward power that resides within the role itself, the more situationally favorable is that position of

Table 3
Measure of Position Power

Below is an 18-item checklist which contains various indices of position power. Simply answer or check only those items which you believe are "true." Skip or do not check any items you do not believe are "true."

_____ 1. Compliments from the leader are appreciated more than compliments from other group members.
_____ 2. Compliments are highly valued, criticisms are considered damaging.
_____ 3. Leader can recommend punishments and rewards.
_____ 4. Leader can punish or reward members on his [or her] own accord.
_____ 5. Leader can effect (or can recommend) promotion or demotion.
_____ 6. Leader chairs or coordinates group but may or may not have other advantages, i.e., is appointed or acknowledged chairman or leader.
_____ 7. Leader's opinion is accorded considerable respect and attention.
_____ 8. Leader's special knowledge or information (and member's lack of it) permits leader to decide how task is to be done or how group is to proceed.
_____ 9. Leader cues members or instructs them on what to do.
_____10. Leader tells or directs members what to do or what to say.
_____11. Leader is expected to motivate group.
_____12. Leader is expected to suggest and evaluate the members' work.
_____13. Leader has superior or special knowledge about the job, or has special instructions but requires members to do the job.
_____14. Leader can supervise each member's job and evaluate it or correct it.
_____15. Leader knows his [or her] own as well as members' job and could finish the work himself [or herself] if necessary, e.g., writing a report for which all information is available.
_____16. Leader enjoys special or official rank and status in real life which sets him [or her] apart from or above group members, e.g., military rank or elected office in a company or organization. (+5 points).
_____17. Leader is given special or official rank by experimenter to simulate for role-playing purposes, e.g., "You are a general" or "the manager." This simulated rank must be clearly superior to members' rank and must not be just that of "chairman" or "group leader" of the group during its work period. (+3 points)
_____18. Leader's position is dependent on members; members can replace or depose leader. (−5 points)

From *Theory of Leader Effectiveness* (p. 24) by F. E. Fiedler, 1967, New York: McGraw Hill. Copyright 1967 by McGraw-Hill publishers. Reprinted by permission.

leadership. This is the least influential situational factor of the three. You may want to complete Table 3 to determine the favorability of your position power.

The degree of a leader's position power is scored by the above scale in which all "true" or checked items are given 1 point except for items 16, 17, and 18 which are weighted +5, +3, and −5 points, respectively. The higher the sum of these scores, the greater is the position power of leadership.

These three situational factors combine to determine the situational favorability of a given leadership position. Given that each of the three variables (leader–member relations, task structure, and position power) could be favorable or unfavorable for the leader, they can be combined in eight ways (see Table 4). For example, the most favorable situation is depicted in the first row of Table 4 (Octant I) where leader–member relations are good, the task is highly structured, and position power is strong. The situations described in the remaining rows are progressively more negative as you read down the table (Fiedler, 1967).

Style-situation. In the last column of Table 4 is the leadership style expected to be most effective within the situation described (Fiedler, 1971). When conditions are very favorable or very unfavorable, a low LPC, task-oriented leader is most effective. In moderately favorable conditions, the relations-oriented, high LPC is an effective leader. Hence, the leadership style that is most effective is contingent upon the interpersonal and organizational characteristics of the situation.

Table 4
A Contingency Model for Effective Leadership

| Octant | Situational Favorability | | | Leadership Style |
	Leader–Member Relations	Task Structure	Position Power	LPC
I	Good	Clear	Strong	Low
II	Good	Clear	Weak	Low
III	Good	Unclear	Strong	Low
IV	Good	Unclear	Weak	High
V	Moderately poor*	Clear	Strong	High
VI	Moderately poor*	Clear	Weak	High
VII	Moderately poor*	Unclear	Strong	Low
VIII	Moderately poor*	Unclear	Weak	Low

From *Theory of Leadership Effectiveness* by F. E. Fiedler, 1967, New York: McGraw-Hill. Copyright 1967 by McGraw-Hill publishers. Reprinted by permission.
*Moderately poor—effective leadership cannot take place with very poor leader–member relations.

Research Findings

As we have seen, contingency theory describes eight different conditions (or octants) of effective leadership by combining two levels of leader–member relations (good or moderately poor), task structure (clear or unclear), and position power (strong or weak). Few studies have attempted to examine each of these octants within the same experimental procedure, but there are a few which did.

For example, in an early study, Fiedler (1966) studied three-man temporary work groups in the Belgium Navy. Half these groups were lead by a petty officer who was given task instructions and final decision making power (strong position power). Half the groups within each of these two divisions worked on the unstructured task of composing a recruiting letter. The remainder completed the structured task of mapping a shipping route.

Before the study began, all leaders completed the LPC scale to assess their leadership style. When the groups had finished their assigned tasks, they rated the atmosphere of the group. This supplied the measure of leader–member relations. In this way, the eight rows in Table 4 were created by the experimental manipulations.

Fiedler (1966) found a configuration of results that was consistent with the general predictions of the contingency model. In general, group performance was highest when low-LPC leaders were matched with very favorable and somewhat unfavorable situations. Relations-oriented, high-LPC leaders were most effective under moderately favorable conditions.

One surprise finding is that position power proved to be more potent than anticipated. The difference between seasoned petty officers averaging 10 years of naval experience and young, untrained recruits may have artificially inflated the significance of this variable. Additionally, only officers were permitted to give instructions, and they had the final say in all decision making. Both factors may have elevated the importance of position power in this study. Generally, position power may be of greater importance in formal, hierarchical organizations, such as the military, than it is in other settings.

A second military study was conducted by Chemers and Skrzypek (1972) at the U.S. Military Academy at West Point. Cadets were assigned to good or moderately poor leader–member groups according to previously administered questionnaires concerned with group atmosphere. They worked on both structured (converting blueprints from metric units to inches) and unstructured (discussion and policy recommendations) tasks. For half the groups, the leaders' position power was strengthened by telling group members that the leaders would evaluate followers' performances and that these ratings would be used by Academy officials to evaluate each individual's standing. The position power of leaders in the remaining groups was not similarly enhanced. The findings supported the predictions of the contingency model for high- and low-LPC leaders.

In a third study that followed the same general pattern outlined in the two previous studies, Graen, Orris, and Alvares (1971) found mixed support for the contingency model with undergraduate students. In two parallel experiments (which differed only in the specific structured and unstructured tasks used) support for contingency predictions was weak. In the first study, only two experimental outcomes differed from what was anticipated, while in the second study, five discrepancies between observed and expected results were found. These findings call into question both the predictive power of the contingency model and the stability of its findings.

Methodological and empirical limitations. The failure of the third study to consistently support the contingency model is only one of many criticisms levied against this body of research. In each of these three studies, none of the findings reached statistical significance. This is due in part to the very large sample of subjects required to test this theory. With eight different conditions to manipulate and small groups of at least three persons the number of subjects needed to conduct a study quickly multiplies. Yet, to separately study octants opens researchers to questions about the legitimacy of comparing findings from different times, places, subjects, and researchers who may use different operational definitions of the three situational variables. For these reasons when all eight octants are studied simultaneously, the number of leaders within each condition is necessarily small, making the achievement of statistical significance exceedingly difficult.

Arguing that statistical significance is an impractical standard against which to judge his model, Fiedler (1966) sought to interpret the configuration of findings across the eight octants. Yet, even this criterion is disappointing. Of the 40 outcomes reported across these three studies, 14 of them were opposite to the predicted direction (Ashour, 1973).

Conclusion. Reporting research summaries gets confusing at times and often becomes highly technical both statistically and methodologically. The safest conclusion from a theoretical standpoint is to say that the evidence is mixed. For the practitioner, on the other hand, this is a very unsatisfactory conclusion.

There are several areas where the evidence is more clear-cut. First, low-LPC leaders clearly were more effective than high-LPC leaders when the leaders themselves described leader–member relations favorably (in 23 of 26 studies, or 88%, Rice, 1976). There is no clear pattern when leaders describe relations as poor.

Second, when leaders' effectiveness is measured by superiors' evaluations and not by group performance the evidence is consistent with contingency predictions (Rice, 1978b). Supervisors positively evaluated both subordinate, low-LPC leaders in conditions that were favorable and moderately unfavorable and high-LPC leaders working in moderately favorable circumstances.

Application

Fiedler's (1966) study with Belgium naval petty officers and recruits raised an important point for practitioners of leadership. In this study, no differences in group performance were found for groups lead by inexperienced recruits and seasoned petty officers. Although the position power of each contributed to the situational favorability experienced by these leaders and hence determined the octant, group performance was affected somewhat by the degree of match between leaders' style and the situational favorability, not by the experience of the leader itself. In general, evaluations of leadership training have yielded disappointing results (Campbell, Dunnette, Lawler, & Weick, 1970).

Fiedler reasoned that to groom effective leaders, training is inadequate, and since LPC is stable, changing the orientation of leaders themselves also is not viable. Effective leadership then rests, not in the individual leader, but rather in (a) the degree of fit between leaders' style and situational favorability, or (b) the mismatched leaders' ability to alter the situational circumstances. The first solution is handled by knowledgeable personnel assignment having assessed the LPC of prospective leaders and the conditions of that particular situation. The second solution may be accomplished through a program dubbed Leader-Match (Fiedler, Chemers, & Mahar, 1976).

Participants in the Leader-Match program read a manual in a 4-to-8-hour period that, in essays and short problems, helps leaders: (a) interpret their LPC score; (b) diagnose their situational control; and (c) modify the situation to bring about a favorable match of leader's style with the situation. Note that the emphasis is on affecting one's situational control. This is accomplished primarily by altering one's position power and the task structure.

For example, the contingency model tells us that high-LPC leaders are most effective in moderately favorable situations. Assuming good leader–member relations, this means that the high-LPC leader should lead groups working on unstructured tasks and should minimize position power (refer to Table 4). The high-LPC leader may do this by requesting unusual, nonroutine tasks and by socializing regularly with group members.

On the other hand, the low-LPC leader faced with the same favorable leader–member relations may clearly structure tasks or if the task must remain unstructured, this leader may strengthen his or her position power. The latter can be accomplished by minimizing informal contact with followers and by requiring that followers schedule appointments.

Although Fiedler and his colleagues do not support on-the-job experience and training for the ideal or normative situation, they do regard training in the form of the Leader-Match program as the way to enhance effective leadership. Some support for the Leader-Match program is offered by contingency theorists. For example, 12 validation studies in civilian (e.g., police sergeants, middle managers, and volunteers) and military (e.g., army infantry platoons and ROTC cadets) settings reported improved supervisors' ratings of leaders' performance after Leader-Match training (Fiedler & Mahar, 1979).

Evaluation

Think about the job that you do. Which octant in the contingency model describes your work? In the laboratory, it is relatively easy to develop a structured and unstructured task and to manipulate position power. In field studies or real-life applications, deciding if a task is clearly structured and rating position power are subjective processes and can lead to different conclusions about the projected LPC of an effective leader. Even in the Leader-Match program, which helps leaders evaluate the amount of situational control they exert, little help is given with the more elusive evaluation of leader–member relations. Additionally, one easily can question the validity of the leader's biased judgment of each of these factors.

Fiedler argues that LPC is a stable personality characteristic and retesting of individuals supports this conclusion. However, leadership is dynamic; it changes over time. It is possible that situational influences may alter the leaders' style over time and hence change their LPC score (Kerr & Harlan, 1973; Ashour, 1973). Repeating testing may show stability because there are no relevant leadership experiences intervening between testings; these experiences, which are part of the true leadership process, indeed may affect Fiedler's model.

The same may be true for the situational variables. Consider the high-LPC leader who has moderately poor leader–member relations and then tries to enact Octant V by structuring tasks and strengthening position power (see Table 4). If this leader is successful, his or her effectiveness will increase. If this happens, leader–member relations may improve. The leader then is no longer in Octant V; rather, the situational favorability becomes that of Octant I, which matches low, not high, LPC leadership. This vicious cycle could continue indefinitely.

The most vulnerable aspect of situational favorability to criticism is leader–member relations. Since one practical application of contingency theory is to match leaders with situations through knowledgeable hiring, personnel officers need to be able to assess leader–member relations *before* they exist. Although the history of these relations may shed some light on the form they will take, this is a far cry from being able to predict what they will be in reality.

In a study described earlier, Chemers and Skrzypek (1972) devised one of the few studies in which leader–member relations could be predicted prior to group formation. West Point cadets were asked to list three peers whom they liked and considered easy to work with as well as three fellow cadets whom they disliked and with whom they preferred not to work. In forming task groups, these experiments were able to assign positively rated followers to one group, and hence assured positive leader–member relations. Groups of cadets rated negatively by the leader helped guarantee poor leader–member relations.

Most personnel workers do not enjoy this flexibility and foreknowledge. The scenerio described still assumes that the appointed leader and followers interact at some time. Furthermore, the transfer of workers to form homogeneous groups is not always realistic. In the most common personnel case, a leader is appointed to head groups that are already formed. Now, leader–member relations cannot be predicted. However, after some time, they can be assessed and the changes suggested by the Leader-Match program may be enacted. Again, as with the other situational variables, the stability of leader–member relations over time cannot be assumed.

The strongest positive aspect of the contingency model is its precision. Leadership style is quickly measured and easily scored. The three factors that define situational favorability are outlined clearly, although leader–member relations may be difficult to accurately observe and classify. For researchers, this ambiguity is less devastating as they can measure leaders' and members' perceptions of group atmosphere at the conclusion of the study.[3] The clarity of contingency theory has made it easy to test, and it has been an influential theory in generating large numbers of research projects. Given all this attention, it is no wonder that its flaws and inadequacies have been discovered. Although the contingency model is repeatedly under attack, it is not yet time to surrender. Peace may be found in a compromise solution.

Using Stodgill's (1974) four criteria for a comprehensive theory, the contingency model fills the gap left by trait and situational theories by dealing with the social context in which leaders' personality is most effective. The theory does not cover how leaders emerge, maintain their status, or relate to changing group processes. It is this emphasis on dynamic, fluid group processes that highlights our final theory of transactional leadership.

A TRANSACTIONAL APPROACH TO LEADERSHIP: LEADER–FOLLOWER EXCHANGE

Definition

Leadership is a dynamic process of mutual influence between a leader and followers directed toward the attainment of mutually established goals that

---

[3]This approach has its pitfalls, because ratings taken at the end of the experiment may be influenced by the success or failure experienced by the leader and group members who have worked together on some task (Ashour, 1973).

maximize benefits and minimize costs for each party. Leadership is a dynamic process; it changes over time as a leader emerges or is appointed and then works within a changing social and physical environment to achieve constantly evolving goals. Leadership is transactional; it reflects the interaction or mutual influence of leaders and followers. Leadership is goal-directed; its purpose is to work toward goals set and changed through group interaction. Finally, leadership is reflective of social exchange; leaders supply rewards and reduce costs for followers in exchange for a favorable balance of rewards and costs for themselves.

Background

The transactional theory of leadership is rooted within the broader theory of social exchange (Homans, 1958, 1961). Applied to interpersonal interaction such as the exchange between leaders and followers, social exchange theory stresses the interdependence of both participants (Thibaut & Kelley, 1959). Each party will remain in the relationship to the extent that it is beneficial to do so. When the costs of the exchange relationship exceed the rewards, the relationship will be terminated. Hence, a leader will emerge and maintain the leadership of the group only when it is advantageous for both the leader and group members.

Equity theory is a type of exchange theory applied to those cases where a person must allocate fairly limited resources. Since leaders frequently function as allocators, equity may be a norm followed by the leader and expected by the followers. Simply stated, equity theorists define a fair exchange as one in which the ratio of inputs to outcomes of both parties are similar (Adams, 1965). For example, leaders who follow the equity rule would give many rewards to hard workers (high inputs/high outcomes) and little to group members who contribute little (low inputs/low outcomes). Equally hard-working parties would merit equal rewards. These relationships are "fair" because everyone "gets what he or she deserves."

The assumption of exchange and equity theories is that individuals and groups seek to maximize profits (rewards minus costs). Relationships are developed and maintained to the extent that they are profitable (or at least, not too costly). Both theories emphasize an exchange between parties and consequent interdependency. It is upon this process of exchange that transactional theory is built.

Theory

The contingency model clearly specifies the components of the situation which interact with leadership style to produce effective leadership. This clarity opened contingency theory to rigorous experimentation. In contrast, a body of research that was generated by transactional theory itself does not exist to any large extent. Transactional theory is a merger of several perspectives and research findings to create an internally consistent, meaningful whole. While contingency theory is a model from which testable hypotheses are deduced, transactional theory seems to be an explanation induced from research and perspectives already published.

Most importantly, the emphasis of transactional theory is upon leader–follower interaction or transaction within a mutually created situation, rather than a combination of leader and situational factors, only one of which is interpersonal. Finally, leadership is defined as a function (what the leader does) or as a role (in the spirit of situational theory) by transactional theorists in contrast with the orientation toward leaders' style (which is more closely aligned with trait theory) exhibited by Fiedler and his colleagues (Burns, 1978; Hollander, 1958, 1978).

The complexities of transactional leadership are depicted in Figure 1. The locus or focal point of leadership occurs where the influence of the situation, followers, and the leader overlap (Hollander, 1978). It is this area of overlap or transaction that is shown in Figure 1. As the double-headed arrows in Figure 1 indicate, the influence of each of these three components (leader, followers, and situation) is circular. To explain the figure, it is necessary to break into the circle at some point—which then becomes both a starting and ending point.

Since followers are an element previous theories have ignored, break the circle at this point. Followers, as individuals and as an interacting unit of individuals, develop expectations about both the situation in which the group functions and the role of the leader. Followers also think of themselves as possessing certain personality characteristics and, in turn, the leader holds certain ideas about the qualities of these followers (Hollander, 1978). For example, members of an academic department may regard the situation as informal with the goal of teaching students and the leader role as that of a laissez-faire administrator. They may think of themselves as competent pro-

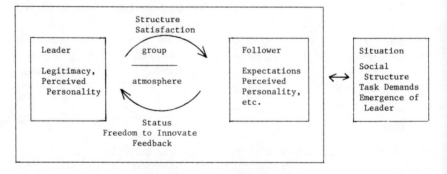

Figure 1.   Locus of leadership.

fessionals while the leader, or department head, may think of them as incompetent administrators. The entire group dynamic will change if the faculty alters its goals to be a researching rather than teaching body.

The second ingredient, the leader, is best defined as the leader role, rather than some configuration of personality characteristics, traits, or style. The leader role is developed through the collaboration of the leader with followers. This role is afforded some degree of legitimacy based on the needs and expectations of followers and the demands of the situation. It is filled by a leader whom followers believe possesses certain qualities, most importantly, competence and motivation to enact group goals (Hollander & Julian, 1969). As goals, expectancies, or tasks change, so does the leader's role.

Note that it is person perception that is the key factor, not the actual traits or style of both leaders and followers. Leaders are judged to be competent to the extent that they appear successful (Jacobs, 1971). Impression management, that is, influencing how one is viewed by others, becomes an important part of maintaining leadership (Goffman, 1959).

In addition to leaders and followers, the leadership dynamic is affected by the process of mutual influence indicated by the two unidirectional arrows. Leaders influence followers and, in turn, are influenced by these same followers. Leaders influence followers by providing (a) structure and (b) satisfaction.

Leaders give structure or direction to the group in both instrumental and normative ways. Instrumentally, leaders (a) clarify what is expected of followers, (b) outline how to meet these expectations; (c) spell out the criteria for evaluating group performance; (d) provide feedback concerning how well individuals or the group are meeting objectives; and (e) allocate rewards and resources (Bass, 1981, p. 263). In sum, leaders manage tasks.

Leaders also help define social reality by contributing to the development of group norms (Hollander & Julian, 1969). Norms are general expectations about how group members should think and act. In this way, leaders have a normative function. Leaders also contribute to the satisfaction of group members. In other words, leaders have two basic functions: to initiate structure and enhance member satisfaction (consideration). The *behavior* of leaders again falls into these two well-studied categories.

In return, followers influence the leader. The followers grant status to the position of leadership, giving the leader role legitimacy. Followers also give the leader the freedom to be innovative, which means that the leader may deviate from group norms at times (Thibaut & Riecken, 1955). Hollander (1958) proposed that leaders conform to group norms when they are campaigning for the leader role. Once that role is secure, the leader has built up a store of idiosyncracy credits which can be spent at critical times. If these deviations and the subsequent debits subtracted from support for the leader lead to success for the group, the leader will have invested wisely and will profit in the long run. When innovations continually fail and debits mount, the leader may no longer enjoy a firm basis from which to continue exercising influence.

Followers give the leader the ability to influence them by complying with the decisions of the leader. This is where the difference between influence and power is clearest. Power resides in one person's ability to unilaterally affect the behaviors of others. On the other hand, influence is a two-way process. A leader is able to influence followers only to the extent that they are willing to be influenced (Hollander, 1964). Finally, followers supply the leader with feedback regarding his or her performance (Bass, 1976b; Likert, 1967). Note the importance of the social exchange process in this pattern of mutual influence. Each party is dependent upon the other; neither works in isolation.

Within this cycle of mutual influence, leaders and followers create and share a common group atmosphere. This atmosphere includes mutual trust, a shared assumption that fairness is achieved through equity, and common information. The transaction of the leader with followers is developed and maintained in interaction with the situation. The situation includes social structure and rules, task demands, and the pattern of emergence of leaders. Social structure involves the characteristics of the group—whether it is formal or informal, hierarchical or flat, centralized or decentralized, and so on. Furthermore, the nature of the task (structured or unstructured, manual or mental, etc.) makes demands of the group. How a leader emerges influences the leadership dynamic. As we shall see shortly, the leadership process differs when leaders are appointed and when they are elected by followers.

The situation influences and is influenced by the leader–follower transaction. For example, if the situation is formal and hierarchical, as in the military, leaders and followers will interact in certain ways. Followers may expect authoritative, directive leadership and effective leaders will comply by actively designing and assigning tasks. These expectations of followers and subsequent behaviors of effective leaders then will reinforce the hierarchical, formal nature of the situation. The two-way cycle of influence or transaction is functioning again.

In sum, leadership is a delicately balanced exchange process. This process is developed and can be changed by followers, the leader, and the situation; this affects the leader-follower transaction. Followers may alter their expectations of the leader who, to remain effective, alters his or her influencing behaviors. These changes finally redefine the situation, and so the cycle continues. Leadership is dynamic, constantly changing, and evolving.

Research Findings

We are accustomed to thinking of leaders' impact upon group members. The influence of followers upon leaders, once an election is over, is less apparent.

Yet, transactional theorists view the influence of followers upon leaders as a critical element of leader–member relations. Since this point is so central to transactional theory, let us look at how followers affect leaders' emergence and behavior.

Candidates for the leader's role are more likely to be successful if they talk a lot in group discussions. High participation calls attention to prospective leaders and convinces the group of the speakers' motivation (Gintner & Lindskold, 1975; Sorrentino & Boutillier, 1975). Furthermore, the person who begins a group discussion is likely to emerge as the leader (Bass, McGehee, Hawkins, Young, & Gebel, 1953).

The emergence of leaders can be stimulated as well as discouraged by the amount of personal acceptance offered by group members. Followers' encouragement can modify leader behavior. In an experiment by Pepinsky, Hemphill, and Shevitz (1958), the degree to which male college students spoke out and initiated structure in groups was assessed in a pretest. Later, these same students took part in discussion groups arranged by the experimenter. When group members supported the suggestions of students who were originally passive, these students began to act leaderlike. The reverse was found for initially assertive students. When these students were confronted by a nonsupportive group, their leader behavior declined significantly. Parallel results were found when the experimenters used signal lights to inform subjects of the degree to which other participants supposedly evaluated their contributions (Zdep & Oakes, 1967).

The behaviors exhibited by established leaders also are affected by the characteristics of followers. In one experiment, secretaries were trained to appear either competent or incompetent (Lowin & Craig, 1968). Supervisors were more considerate and imposed less structure upon competent secretaries than they did upon incompetent ones.

In a second study, subordinates were trained to play the role of democratic or autocratic followers. Democratic subordinates set their own goals and generated ideas, while autocratic group members asked for instructions which they followed without question. Male management students leading these groups exhibited different leadership behaviors consistent with the role played by group members. Leadership indeed is a two-way process. Leaders influence followers who in turn influence them. Furthermore, the nature of influence changes over time as the group and the situation in which it functions continually change.

Application

Transactional theory offers several practical suggestions for persons wishing to become and remain the leader of a group (Hollander, 1978, pp. 53—60). As we have seen, an important component of emerging leadership is high participation in group discussion, especially in problem-solving groups. Visibility, commitment, and motivation are assumed to underlie high rates of participation (quantity), regardless of the ability (quality) reflected in this participation.

In addition to high participation, emerging leaders should concentrate on enhancing their legitimacy in the eyes of followers. In other words, an emerging leader should persuade followers that he or she is the right person for the job. Often, this can be accomplished subtly through nonverbal cues. For example, the emerging leader may take a seat at the head of a table. The point is to do leaderlike things.

How leaders achieve legitimacy is dependent upon the processes through which they are emerging. Appointed leaders may not readily enjoy the support of their followers in the way that elected leaders do. Circumstances will be most favorable for appointed leaders, if followers believe that the appointment resulted from the proven competence of the appointee (Goldman & Fraas, 1965).

Often, elected leaders enjoy greater latitude in their initial decision making (Hollander, Fallon, & Edwards, 1977). Elected leaders pay a price for this support in the form of higher expectations from followers and greater accountability (Lamm, 1973). Elected leaders will argue a case in front of outsiders harder than appointed ones because of this perceived accountability to the desires of group members. The most favorable conditions for leadership are for the leader to emerge and then be elected (Firestone, Lichtman, & Colamosca, 1975). The high participation and apparent motivation reflected in emergence, combined with the legitimacy and support of a winning vote, help these leaders get tasks done.

Once leaders have emerged, their concerns shift to remaining in office. The focus of leaders changes to: (a) having followers recognize them as competent and motivated (Alvarez, 1968); (b) fullfilling role expectations for consideration and structure; (c) adapting to changing situational demands, and (d) accountability.

Accountability of leaders is recorded in an imaginary ledger of debits and idiosyncracy credits. This is where insiders and outsiders differ. Leaders who have emerged from the group's membership have established credits upon which they can draw. Leaders who come from an outside source may simultaneously pose a threat and engender envy among insiders as well as bring opportunities for a fresh start and the promise of successes achieved elsewhere. The ledger of outsiders is less solid than that of insiders. As a relatively unknown quantity, the outside leader will need some time to develop an account of social exchange costs and benefits.

A key ingredient in maintaining leadership is open communication with followers (Klauss & Bass, 1981). This enhances the leader–follower transaction which is an essential component of the leadership dynamic. Communication contributes to the leader's influence on followers' satisfaction, fullfilling role expectations dealing with consideration. It also recognizes the account-ability the leader feels toward followers. Effective communication between supervisors and workers has been shown to improve productivity (Hain, 1972), increase efficiency, reduce grievances, and lower absenteeism (Hain & Tubbs, 1974).

Evaluation

In terms of Stodgill's (1974) criteria for a comprehensive theory of lead-ership, transactional theory deals with the emergence and maintenance of leadership. In its emphasis on leader–follower relations, transactional theory seems to be strongest where contingency theory is most lacking. Although transactional theorists recognize the importance of situational variables, they do not define these factors as clearly as contingency theorists do. Perhaps an eclectic merger of these two approaches may yield a more complete picture of leaders' effectiveness.

The dynamics of transactional theory are both a strength and a weakness. Surely, the demands placed upon leaders change over time. The expert campaigner is not necessarily the most effective leader. One form of lead-ership may be effective in times of crisis; other styles may be demanded in more placid circumstances. The changing fluid nature of leadership is cap-tured by transactional theory.

On the other hand, the continual change described by transactional theo-ry inhibits adequate experimental examination. Fiedler offered three situa-tional variables that researchers easily could identify and manipulate. Upon what factors would a transactional theorist concentrate? The answer is less straighforward. This vagueness also hinders the practitioner. How do you train an effective leader, if the circumstances are changing continually? Is leadership commonsensical with a large dose of "playing it by ear?" Transac-tional theory gives this impression and indeed this view may reflect reality. Although transactional theorists do offer "a practical guide to effective lead-ership" (Hollander, 1978), the advice given is less clear-cut than that found in the Leader-Match program. Good theories should be simple and par-simonious as well as reflective of reality (useful). The trade-offs in achieving both of these standards can be seen in a comparison of the more complex transactional theory with the contingency model.

SUMMARY

In this chapter, we have reviewed four approaches to examining leadership. None of these four perspectives is comprehensive if it stands alone. However, an eclectic overview of all four theories paints a fuller picture. Trait theories sketch the leader and the characteristics he or she brings to the group portrait. Situational theories paint in the background, reflecting the social context in which leadership takes place. The contingency model molds these two perspectives into the same picture, making sure that the artistic form and colors blend. Finally, transactional theory fills in the followers, again concentrating on achieving aesthetic harmony by blending the influence of followers with that of both leaders and the situation. For the transactional theorists, this paints only one stationary frame of a movie. The story of leadership processes unfolds over time as the changing frames of the movie pass through the projector.

So far, we have seen that leadership is regarded as a process of mutual influence: leaders influence followers who are in turn influenced by group members. This mutual exchange takes place within a situational context which also influences the processes or transaction of leadership. In the next chapter, we will take a closer look at leadership as an influence process.

Chapter 2

Leadership As An Influence Process

In chapter 1, we discussed the various approaches to the understanding of leadership. As we saw, our knowledge of leadership evolved historically, examining who leaders were, how they behaved, and what roles or situations they assumed or operated. In that discussion the emphasis was on the leader as a person. As you will see in this chapter, we will discuss leadership as a process between the leader and those who are led. Although the leader may have power, influence may depend more on persuasion than on legitimate, formal positions. A leadership process involves some two-way influence in the relationship. Moreover, it is aimed at attaining mutual goals. In other words, leadership has been considered as the focus of influence by which an organization can obtain its formal goals. On behalf of followers, the leader is the person through whose influence followers can satisfy their personal needs while pursuing organizational goals.

The term leadership is used freely both in conversation and in writing. There is a great deal of misunderstanding of what is really meant by that term. The leader might be someone who seems larger than life, that is, one who appears to attract others like a magnet or by some form of charisma. The leader may be the person others want to follow—a person who commands trust and respect as well as loyalty. This, of course paints a picture of an emergent leader or, as discussed in the first chapter, the "great man" who captures the imagination as well as the admiration of those with whom the leader must deal. These include presidents, military war commanders, and historical officals. However, most of the world's work is done by leaders who are less heroic. These are supervisors of hospital wards, retail stores, chairpersons of parent–teacher groups, supervisors of assembly lines, department heads, executives in governmental agencies, and the like. Thus, when we talk about leadership, we use the term to encompass the multitude of these supervisors as well as those charismatic and heroic personalities.

Leadership has been studied and researched for a number of years and, of course, there are numerous theories and models. For example, Stogdill

(1974) points out that there are more than 3,000 scholars and researchers who have in some way studied the phenomeon of leadership. No attempt will be made to review these; rather, we will follow the framework set forth in Chapter 1 to examine four often-described approaches to leadership. In this chapter we will define leadership; we will describe how various objective and subjective measures have been obtained; we will identify where attempts have been make to link leadership theory to practice, and where there is a gap we will offer suggestions on ways to improve convergent thought between the study of leadership and how leadership is actually practiced.

LEADERSHIP DEFINED

Theoretical Definitions

Much has been written about the topic of leadership in the past 40 years, resulting in numerous definitions of leadership. However, no universally accepted definition has been developed. Although we will review some definitions early in this chapter, it is with the focus on "influence" that we plan to establish a better foundation to understand leadership.

Homans (1950) introduced the influence of the leader–follower process through a group perspective. He stated that

> Leadership or the leader is the man [sic] who comes closest to realizing the norms the group values highest; this conformity gives him his high rank, which attracts people and implies the right to assume control of the group.

According to Dubin (1951),

> Leadership is the exercise of authority and the making of decisions.

Hemphill (1954) states that

> Leadership is the initiation of acts that result in a consistent pattern of group interactions directed toward the solution of mutual problems.

For Cartwright (1965), leadership was equated to

> a domain of influence.

Katz and Kahn (1966) refine the concept of influence in leadership. They consider

> the essence of organizational leadership to be the influential increment over and above mechanical compliance with routine directions of the organization.

In other words, Katz and Kahn state that although all supervisors at the same level of the organizational hierarchy possess equal formal or legitimate power, they do not all use it with equal effectiveness to influence individuals and the organization. Similarly, Hollander and Julian (1969) suggest that

> Leadership in the broadest sense implies the presence of a particular influence relationship between two or more persons.

According to Bass (1981)

> Effort to change the behavior of others is attempted leadership. When the other members actually change, this creation of change in others is successful leadership. If the others are reinforced or rewarded for changing their behavior, this evoked achievement is effective leadership.

What Bass notes is that the distinction between successful and effective leadership is important, because the dynamics of each are quite different.

The influence concept that underlies many of these definitions recognizes the fact that people differ in the extent to which their activities affect the group. What is implied here is a reciprocal relationship between leaders and followers— not one necessarily characterized by domination and control or induction of compliance on the part of the leader. Simply, it states that leaders exercise a determining effect on the behavior of group members and on the activities of the group. By defining effective leadership as successful influence by the leader that results in goal attainment by compliant followers, leadership is in essence defined by goal attainment. This working definition can be quite useful, because it permits the transfer of theory toward understanding leader and follower relations in practice.

LEADERSHIP: THE PHENOMENON AND THE LEADER

Because leadership is a process and not a person, the outcome or the desired influence may vary in several different settings. Certainly the leader is the pivotal focus of the leadership process. However, followers also are important in this relationship, because without responsive followers there is no leadership. This means that the concept of leadership is relational. It involves someone who exerts influence as well as those who are, in fact, influenced. Influence can go both ways. People other than the appointed leader and the nature of the social setting in which they relate also are necessary aspects of the leadership phenomenon. Some leaders are placed in charge, and their legitimacy is based on appointment. On the other hand, the leader may be someone who has emerged to secure the following of the group. We learned this as a byproduct of the early Hawthorne experiments.

In those experiments from 1927 to 1932, Elton Mayo (1953) and his colleagues from Harvard conducted a series of studies of human behavior in work situations at the Hawthorne plant of Western Electric (Rothlisberger & Dickson, 1939). In a series of experiments, Mayo and his associates divided followers into "test groups" that were subject to deliberate changes in work environment (e.g., illumination, temperature, etc.) and "control groups" whose work environment remained constant during a period in which productivity was measured. For example, when one test group's lighting conditions improved, productivity increased—as expected. However, a similar increase in productivity occurred when lighting was worsened!

In another experiment, Mayo and his Harvard coworkers placed two groups of six women in separate rooms. For one group the work conditions were varied, but in the other they were not. A number of variables were tried: salaries were increased; coffee breaks of varying lengths were introduced; the workday and the work week were shortened. The researchers, who now acted as leaders, allowed the groups to choose their own rest periods and to have a say in other suggested changes. The other group was not able to make these changes.

Once again, output went up in both the test and control groups. The researchers felt they could rule out financial and other incentives as the causes, because the control group was kept to the same payment schedule and work routine. Mayo concluded that a complex psychological, emotional chain reaction had touched off the productivity increases. Because both the test and control groups had been singled out for special attention, they developed a group pride that motivated them to improve their work performance. The sympathetic supervision they both received had further reinforced their increased motivation. The result of this experiment gave Mayo his first important discovery: When special attention is given to workers by management, productivity is likely to increase, regardless of actual changes in working conditions. This phenomenon became known as the Hawthorne effect.

However, one question remained unanswered. Why should special attention plus the formation of group bonds elicit such strong reactions? To find the answer, Mayo launched a massive interview program, which led to this most significant finding: Informal work groups with emergent leaders have a great influence on productivity. Many of the employees found their lives inside and outside the factory dull and meaningless. But their workplace associations, based in part on mutual antagonism toward the "formal leaders" imparted some meaning to their working lives. For this reason, group pressure, rather than formal leadership demands, had the strongest influence on how productive they would be (Mayo, 1953). This less formal process of emergence and these varied kinds of legitimacy depend more on followers than on organizational structure.

Later reviews of the Hawthorne studies have discussed some methodological problems that call into question the validity of these findings (Carey, 1967; Landsberger, 1958). These later studies and reviews seriously jeopardized the "Hawthorne effect." Still, a strong case for the influence of informal group norms on members' performance was demonstrated in another classic study conducted by Coch and French (1948) at the Harwood Corporation. Here, frequent changes in production methods were responsible for high turnover, reduced efficiency, and hostility toward management. Coch and French decided to study three different approaches to instituting production changes to see if participation of work-group members in making changes would reduce the problems previously associated with these changes. In the control group, change was instituted in the usual way: Management simply instructed employees to make changes. In the partial participation groups, elected representatives of the workers consulted with management about proposed changes. In the total participation groups, all workers were able to influence decisions regarding suggested changes.

The findings gave clear support to the hypothesis that employees' participation would contribute to smoothly bringing about production changes. In the control group, production declined and was sustained at a low level. Also, workers' grievances with management increased after the changes were instituted. In contrast, after the changes were made, production initially fell for both participation groups, but then recovered rapidly, coming to a plateau of production higher than the original rates. Most convincingly, Coch and French (1948) later allowed members of the original control group to participate in decision making, and they found that, like the original participation groups, the original control group's production rates fell and then recovered at a level higher than the original. These findings combined with those of the Hawthorne experiments indicate that informal group norms influence group performance.

When leadership is viewed as an influence process, we are better able to understand that leadership involves power relationships. The power relationships may be formal bases of power that result from a position that signals legitimacy, the capacity to reward or punish, or those bases of power that are characterized within the individual, referent and expert. Because power is regarded as a form of influence, it can be observed that some leaders, more than others, tend to transform a leadership opportunity into a successful outcome. Formal organizations have formal structures, and these levels of authority accord people power as a scarce resource. Underlying the sources of social power is the consent from those who allow themselves to be influenced. If the leader is to be effective, those under the leader's charge must grant their consent or respect in order to let the leader influence them.

Therefore, the process of leadership involves a social exchange between the leaders and followers in a given situation. When leaders are effective, they provide something or facilitate the means to obtain something, and of course, the leader obtains something in return. This social exchange, or what Hollander (1978) calls a "transactional approach," involves a trading of benefits. The leader provides a benefit in directing the group toward desired organizational goals, and hopefully, the group supports formal organizational goals. In return, the group members provide the leader with status and privileges of authority. The leader has greater prestige and influence. Such a social exchange applies to situations of appointed leadership or legitimate leadership based upon formal position, as well as to situations with emergent and informal leadership activities.

LEADER–FOLLOWER EXCHANGE

A specific example of the transactional approach to leadership involves an investigation of the exchange between a person in a leader position and one in a follower position. Graen (1976) coined the term *vertical dyad linkages* to examine the development of leader–follower exchange within organizational units. Graen and his associates propose that leadership is a social exchange process by which the leader and a follower work through how each will behave in certain situations, and they also agree upon the general nature of their relationship (e.g., developing norms against the background of the situations they must face in the normal organization, Dansereau, Graen, and Haga, 1975; Graen, 1976; Graen and Cashman, 1975). Thus, these leader–follower exchanges or role development processes produce dyadic (two person) social structures.

The vertical dyad linkage (VDL) approach is used to investigate the development of leader–follower exchanges within organizational units where the parties to the vertical relationships are in the process of working through their respective roles. We can assume that in early social exchanges leaders and followers search for cues of the emerging dyadic social structures. These cues, once discovered, are used to predict over time the nature of the fully developed social structure and the inputs of that structure (Graen & Cashman, 1975).

Consider a hypothetical example to see how this process works. One cue or signal of the emerging dyadic social structure is the negotiating attitude between the leader and a follower. An early sign of the "nature" of the emerging leader–follower exchange is the follower's perception of his or her relationship with the leader as a source of individualized assistance (e.g., reward, coersion, expertise, etc.). Only after a follower comes to view the leader as "open" to dyadic exchanges can the follower be expected to engage in such exchanges. Thus, when a follower perceives that the leader is open to requests for individualized assistance, it is taken as a sign that vertical dyadic negotiation is possible and that an "in-group"exchange is developing. On the other hand, when a follower perceives that the leader is relatively "closed" to requests for individualized assistance, it is taken as a sign that vertical dyadic negotiation is unlikely and that "out-group" exchange is developing (Graen & Cashman, 1975).

What is being described in this in-group, out-group exchange is a description of the role-making processes of leadership. Here is an example of how the vertical dyad works. There is an old adage in the military that a leader is responsible for all things that the unit does or fails to do. Whereas the leader cannot escape the overall responsibility for a group's actions, it is not realistic to assume that the leader personally does everything or even checks everything done by the followers.

Although a leader can delegate important tasks to some members, the leader maintains primary responsibility for the accomplishment of these tasks. If the subordinate fails, so does the leader. Thus, the leader must enlist at least some of the followers as "special" assistants (Vroom, 1976). Graen and Cashman call these followers "in-group" members. The leader tends to select in-group members who are compatible with the leader in terms of work competence and, possibly, interpersonal skills. Perhaps most importantly, the leader selects those followers whom he or she can trust without watching closely.

In addition to the developing social structure, the outputs of that structure are influenced by in-group and out-group transactions with the leader. Graen and Cashman (1975) report that leaders indicate that followers in an in-group status act more consistently with the leader's expectations. Conversely, out-group followers are perceived by leaders as acting progressively more deviant from the leader's expectations; thus, out-group followers deviate more from what the leader wants. In sum, the VDL model posits that leaders differentiate their work units by developing in-group exchanges with selected followers. The result is that the leaders are open to provide individualized assistance, enabling in-group followers to assume greater involvement in activities and receive greater positional resources from the leader than out-group followers do.

For a moment we should pause to consider the theoretical merits of the vertical dyadic linkage model to our better understanding of the phenomenon of leadership and leadership processes. First, we assume that the development of leader–follower social exchange requires the parties to be working through their respective roles and codifying norms. Second, we must also recognize that the vertical relationships are dynamic and require time to develop. In other words, the perceived negotiating attitude in a vertical dyad requires that trust be established before the leader offers greater amounts of positional resources (e.g., sensitive treatment, stronger support, more information, etc.) Such relationships, depending on the degree of interdependence and cohesion, must be developed carefully over an extended period of time. Clearly, then, longitudinal studies provide the best insight to the unfolding process.

A most insightful contribution to leadership theory is the relationship of in-group and out-group exchanges between leaders and followers. The traditional assumption of an "average leader style" is that the leader will develop what Graen (1976) calls homogeneous exchanges with followers. Stated differently, traditional leader–follower transactions assume that all will be in-group exchanges or all out-group exchanges; none will be mixed. The vertical dyad linkage (VDL) model assumes that many relationships will be mixed. This assumption is based on the belief that the leader interacts uniquely with each follower, and thus, there are heterogeneous vertical relationships within organizations.

Implication and Utility of the VDL

The VDL model does not demonstrate any new approach to leadership. In fact, Graen and Cashman (1975, p. 148) stated that "it may be seen as a special case of a class of studies already in the mainstream of leadership." A test of utility of the vertical dyadic linkage model requires that comparisons be made between characteristics of the VDL and more traditional approaches.

One example of these traditional approaches is the "average leadership style" approach, one of the most widely used and most straightforward measurements of contemporary leadership (Fleishman & Simmons, 1970). The assumption, in this instance, is one of a supervisor whose behaviors can be described as varying over relatively few dimensions (two, in most cases). These behavioral patterns are assumed to be stylistic for a particular supervisor and thus applied similarly to all followers. Further, this simplifying assumption is also made regarding the reaction of followers. For example, all subordinates within a unit will respond approximately the same to various levels of consideration or initiating structure. Hence, followers are regarded as a homogeneous group so that their reactions to leadership are averaged.

A more complex approach to understanding the dynamics of leadership has been utilized by a number of other researchers (e.g., House, 1968; House & Kerr, 1973) in an effort to overcome the same major weaknesses of the "average style" approach used by Korman (1966). Graen and Cashman (1975) call this the "mixed model" of leadership behavior. This approach rejects the assumption of the homogeneity of followers' reactions to the leader's behavior. Leaders' behaviors are assumed to be most relevant in their impact upon the psychological states of their subordinates as individuals. Consistent with this assumption, measurement is focused at the level of the individual rather than of the group as a homogeneous whole.

But what about the leader's behavior? The VDL approach also assumes heterogeneous behaviors from both the leader and the followers. Unlike the "average leadership style" approach, the "vertical dyad linkage" (VDL) approach does not assume that leader behavior is consistent across followers or that followers' reactions to it are essentially the same. Rather, the present approach assumes that leaders may act differently toward unit members and that these members may differ in their reactions to the leaders. Therefore, the appropriate level of study is not the work group nor the individual, but the vertical dyad.

In sum, the VDL is a special case of examining leadership as an influence process in social exchange. It fits well in the transactional approach because the focus is neither on the leader nor on the followers as a group but rather the unique vertical dyadic exchange among leaders and followers and the situational constraints which impact on the formation of the dyadic relationship. As will be seen in Chapter 4, the VDL model will be quite instructive as we examine the relative novelty of leader–follower relationships when there are mixed sexes (e.g., male leader, female followers; female leader, male followers; male leader, male followers; and female leader, female followers in masculine sex-typed tasks). Only through the VDL theory can the influence processes that occur in the described relationships be explained.

SEX-ROLES AND SEX DIFFERENCES IN LEADERSHIP

Only in the last 15 years has systematic research on women as leaders been carried out. According to Bender (1979), one research strategy adopted in early studies was to substitute female subjects for male respondents in traditional leadership research designs and measure what occurs. It is not surprising to find, that in general, the leadership process is significantly modified when the group leader is a woman instead of a man.

The changing cultural values concerning roles of women in society coupled with federal legislation banning discrimination on the basis of sex in employment practices have opened many new opportunities for women in what were previously considered to be traditional, male-dominant occupations. Today women are military pilots, law enforcement officials, senior corporate managers, surgeons, and a host of other positions, where less than two decades ago women would have been considered as anomalies. Several scholars of women in leadership report that performance within groups varies because of the sex of the leader (Hollander & Yoder, 1980). And although a continuing growth in the body of literature documents the fact that women are evaluated differently from men as leaders (Rice, Bender, & Vitters, 1980), there is very little evidence in field studies that women in leadership positions behave differently from male leaders in similar roles.

Sex-Roles: Masculinity and Femininity

It is important that we establish a clear understanding of sex-roles and how the term is used in leadership research. According to Mischel (1970), sex-roles are those behaviors that are less expected and sanctioned when performed by one sex and in contrast are considered to be more appropriate when manifested by members of the other sex. For example, in several studies involving sex-roles and leadership, men in our culture are more often described by the following adjectives: independent, aggressive, competitive, self-confident, rational, dominant, and objective. On the other hand, women in the studies are more apt to be described as sympathetic, quiet, gentle, tactful, passive, irrational, and even emotional. Here the terms sex-roles and gender will be used interchangeably to describe stereotypic masculine or feminine roles. We use the term sex differences to denote variance in function due to physiological differences in women and men.

In American culture men are generally perceived as doers and achievers, whereas women are stereotypically perceived as possessing more passive qualities and perhaps greater interpersonal skills. Also, the "feminine personality" is considered as being less appropriate for leader roles. This opinion is easily documented. For example, Brenner (1970) cites a nationwide survey of managers showing that the four personal characteristics rated most important for an upper-management position were considered to be possessed more often by men than women. Bowman, Worthy, and Greyser (1965) found that of 1,000 male executives surveyed, 44% expressed mildly unfavorable to strongly unfavorable attitudes toward women in management. The most frequently cited reason for nonacceptance of women in these roles is the belief that women are "temperamentaily" ill-suited for leadership positions.

As we discussed in the first chapter, Schein (1973) asked 300 male middle managers to rate women in general, men in general, and successful middle managers on 92 descriptive trait items. Schein predicted that successful middle managers would be seen as possessing characteristics and temperaments more commonly ascribed to men in general than to women, and the results supported her predictions. There was a significant relationship between the ratings of men and successful managers; little resemblance was found between the ratings of women and successful managers.

Clearly, there are several implications for these findings concerning sex-roles, sex differences, and leadership. First, it appears that the research on the traits of leaders has developed into what might be considered a masculine-based characterization, one which matches stereotypic attitudes about the ability of women in leadership positions. This is not surprising, given the predominant culture during an era when leadership research focused on leader traits. Indeed, Bender (1979) cites that much of the early literature on leadership was done by men using male subjects. Perhaps this image of a leader, normatively defined by male attributes, has affected previous research.

Also, the number of women in leadership positions even to date is very limited. An investigation of factors which influence the access to leadership becomes important toward understanding the processes that take place with female leaders. Certainly, discrimination based upon societal stereotypes is often listed as a major factor in limiting access of women to leadership roles. Finally, studying women also expands our view of leadership to encompass feminine characteristics, a change that we feel is needed. However, there also may be trait-based personality variables which affect the performance of women. These leadership personality factors may include attributes of psychological masculinity and femininity. We will have much more to say about the influence of these attributes and other traits in leadership as we review longitudinal studies in the chapters to follow.

While men and women possess some distinct physiological differences, they are not necessarily psychologically different. For example, masculine sex-role characteristics like aggressiveness, competitiveness, and self-confidence, are not biological traits unique to one sex. Rather, the distributions of these characteristics for men and women as groups overlap. According to Spence and Helmreich (1978), masculinity or agentic traits are psychological concepts which society has typically ascribed more to men than to women. Conversely, the sex-role characteristics like empathy, gentleness, and passiveness are also psychological concepts which society has ascribed stereotypically more to women than to men. Whereas the nonprofessional might argue that men and women tend to have different sets of life experiences which define sex-roles, evidence from contemporary studies of sex-roles and leadership indicates that men and women with similar education, career aspirations, and training have basically identical scores on measures of psychological masculinity and femininity. (Adams, Priest, & Prince, in press).

How Do You Rate on a Masculinity-Femininity Scale?

For some people, being masculine or feminine is a central aspect of their self-concept. Within the American culture, men are supposed to be masculine, women are supposed to be feminine, and neither sex is supposed to be much like the other. Men are supposed to be tough, dominant, and fearless; women are supposed to be tender, sympathetic, and sensitive to the needs of others. Any man who is highly expressive and shows his emotions visibly by crying is likely to have his masculinity questioned. Similarly, a woman who assertively defends her career as a boxer or construction worker is likely to have her femininity questioned. In American society, masculinity and femininity reflect this bias: A person can score as either masculine or feminine, but most tests do not allow a person to say that he or she is some of both.

According to Bem (1977), a person can be both masculine and feminine. For example, Bem states that a baby can be dressed in pink on Mondays and blue on Tuesdays; a preschooler can be given both trucks and dolls for Christmas; an adolescent can spend some leisure time playing basketball in the driveway and other time serving as a nurse's aide in the local hospital. In principle, a person can also blend, in a single act, these complementary ways of dealing with the world. For example, a person can criticize an employee's job performance straightforwardly but also with sensitivity for possible guilt or anger or distress that such criticism inevitably produces. The concept of androgyny (from the Greek *andro,* male, and *gyne,* female) refers specifically to this blending of the behaviors and personality characteristics that have been traditionally thought of as masculine and feminine. By definition, then, the androgynous individual is someone who is capable of being both independent and dependent, both aggressive and gentle, both assertive and yielding, and both masculine and feminine, depending on the situational appropriateness of these various behaviors (Bem, 1977).

In the next section is a personality inventory called the Personal Attributes Questionnaire (PAQ) scale developed by Spence, Helmreich, and Stapp (1974). It measures a person's self-reported score on masculine or agentic characteristics (high masculine, low feminine), feminine or expressive characteristics (high feminine, low masculine), androgynous characteristics (high masculine, high feminine), and an undifferentiated category (low masculine and low feminine scores). See Table 5.

Scoring the PAQ is accomplished in three steps: First, calculate masculinity and femininity scores for each person. Second, calculate medians for masculinity and femininity scores based upon the total group in the sample (using female and male scores combined). This step may be omitted and median masculinity and femininity scores from the Spence and Helmreich normative group can be used. Finally, classify individuals according to whether their masculinity and femininity scores are above or below each of the two medians identified. The four-way classification may be expanded into an eight-way classification by dividing persons in each of the four cells shown in Table 6 into those falling above or below the median on the Masculinity/ Femininity scale. The eightfold classification typology has particular utility to researchers investigating results from the eightfold schema.

The masculinity and femininity scores are simply the means of the ratings of the masculine and feminine adjectives on the PAQ. That is, a given individual's masculinity score is the mean of that individual's rating on the mas-

Table 5
Personal Attribute Questionnaire

The items below inquire about what kind of a person you think you are. Each items consists of a pair of characteristics, with the letters A–E in between. For example:

Not at all artistic   A   B   C   D   E   Very artistic

Each pair describes contradictory characteristics—that is, you cannot be both at the same time, such as very artistic and not at all artistic. The letters form a scale between the two extremes. You are to choose a letter which describes where you fall on the scale. For example, if you think you have no artistic ability, you would choose A. If you think you are pretty good, you might choose D. If you are only medium, you might choose C, and so forth.

Scale**

M–F	1.	Not at all aggressive	A	B	C	D	E	Very aggressive*
M	2.	Not at all independent	A	B	C	D	E	Very independent*
F	3.	Not at all emotional	A	B	C	D	E	Very emotional*
M–F	4.	Very submissive	A	B	C	D	E	Very dominant*
M–F	5.	Not at all excitable* in a major crisis	A	B	C	D	E	Very excitable in a major crisis
M	6.	Very passive	A	B	C	D	E	Very active*
F	7.	Not at all able to devote self completely to others	A	B	C	D	E	Able to devote self completely to others*
F	8.	Very rough	A	B	C	D	E	Very gentle*
F	9.	Not at all helpful to others	A	B	C	D	E	Very helpful to others*
M	10.	Not at all competitive	A	B	C	D	E	Very competitive*
M–F	11.	Very home-oriented	A	B	C	D	E	Very worldly*
F	12.	Not at all kind	A	B	C	D	E	Very kind*
M–F	13.	Indifferent to others' approval*	A	B	C	D	E	Highly needful of others' approval
M–F	14.	Feelings not easily hurt*	A	B	C	D	E	Feelings easily hurt
F	15.	Not at all aware of feelings of others	A	B	C	D	E	Very aware of feelings of others*
M	16.	Can make decisions easily*	A	B	C	D	E	Has difficulty making decisions
M	17.	Gives up very easily	A	B	C	D	E	Never gives up easily*
M–F	18.	Never cries	A	B	C	D	E	Cries very easily*
M	19.	Not at all self-confident	A	B	C	D	E	Very confident*
M	20.	Feels very inferior	A	B	C	D	E	Feels very superior*
F	21.	Not at all understanding of others	A	B	C	D	E	Very understanding of others*
F	22.	Very cold in relations with others	A	B	C	D	E	Very warm in relations with others*
M–F	23.	Very little need for security*	A	B	C	D	E	Very strong need for security
M	24.	Goes to pieces under pressure	A	B	C	D	E	Stands up well under pressure*

From *Masculinity & Femininity* by J. T. Spence and R. L. Helmreich, 1978, Austin, TX: University of Texas Press. Copyright 1978 by J. T. Spence & R. L. Helmreich. Reprinted by permission.

*The asterisk above a word choice indicates the extreme masculine response for the M and M–F scales and the extreme feminine response for the F scale. Each extreme masculine response on the M and M–F scales and extreme feminine response on the F scale are scored 4, the next most extreme scored 3, etc.

**The scale to which each item is assigned is indicated below by M (Masculinity), F (Femininity), and M–F (Masculinity–Femininity).

Table 6
Framework for Classifying Persons on Masculinity and Femininity Scores

Femininity	Masculinity	
	Above Median	Below Median
Above Median	Androgynous	Feminine
Below Median	Masculine	Undifferentiated

From *Masculinity and Femininity* (p. 35) by J. T. Spence and R. L. Helmreich, 1978, Austin, TX: University of Texas Press. Copyright by J. T. Spence & R. L. Helmreich. Reprinted by permission.

culine adjectives, and that same individual's femininity score is the mean of his or her ratings on the feminine adjectives. The placement of adjectives on the PAQ is as follows:

1. The adjectives used to measure androgyny are items 1, 4, 5, 11, 13, 14, 18, and 23.
2. The adjectives used to measure masculinity are items 2, 6, 10, 16, 17, 19, 20, and 24.
3. The adjectives used to measure femininity are items 3, 7, 8, 9, 12, 15, 21, and 22.

Once each person's masculinity and femininity scores have been calculated in this way, the median masculinity score and the median femininity score for the particular group then must be calculated. The median masculinity score is that score above which 50% of the masculinity scores fall; the median femininity score is that score above which 50% of the femininity scores fall. Ideally, the scores of both males and females should be considered together when these two medians are calculated, and, if unequal numbers of males and females are involved, the numbers should be equalized statistically by weighting the underrepresented sex by an appropriate amount.

Although it would be best to calculate medians in this manner, this may not be possible in certain situations. In such cases, it is possible to use the normed medians as developed by Spence and Helmreich using data from 715 college students. To obtain the median values for the masculinity, femininity, and androgyny scales, the reader is asked to contact the scale authors. Spence and Helmreich note that strict comparability across samples is compromised by using different norms. Therefore, we recommend that relationships within a given population sampled would be more clearly illustrated by using medians derived from that population.

Looking at the PAQ scale, one should note that a psychological sex-role orientation need not be the same as your biological sex. For example, a man may score high on the femininity scale and low on the masculinity scale. This man, then, would be classified as psychologically feminine. Furthermore, this classification is not related to our hypothetical man's sexual preference. Psychological masculinity, femininity, and androgyny, sexual preference, and biological sex (male or female) may overlap, but they are not completely, clearly related. Our example may be biologically male, psychologically feminine, and sexually heterosexual. Understanding the differences among these three concepts (sex-role orientation, physiological sex, and sexual preference) is a first step toward comprehending sex roles and their influence on the leaders' role.

Biological Sex and Attributions of Performance

A popular theme in leadership research in the past few years has been to examine the influence of biological sex with leadership in masculine, sex-typed tasks. For example, in male-dominant leadership positions, similar performance by males and females is perceived to be caused by different elements. Successful male performance is more often attributed to internal factors related to the person's disposition, such as skill and ability. Successful female performance is more often attributed to external factors related to the situation, such as luck or, perhaps, the simplicity of the task.

According to Deaux and Emswiller (1974), our choice of explanations for causes of performance is influenced by our prior beliefs about people. To illustrate this belief, a laboratory experiment was designed which allowed the investigators to measure the amount of influence that sex contributes to the process of leadership. The experiment required that judges evaluate the performance of male and female leaders who performed a variety of tasks. When the work was considered to be stereotypically masculine, judges explained skill as the cause of successful performance by men. But the same judges viewed luck as the cause of successful performance on the same tasks by women leaders. Even though the judges saw identical evidence of male and female leader performance, they found different explanations. Clearly, expectations concerning the sex of the leader (not necessarily the characteristics of the leader per se) seem to be an important element when people evaluate female leaders in male-dominant roles. Regrettably, no comprehensive theory of leadership or model of leadership has attempted to illustrate the relational aspects of sex-roles and sex-differences in leadership, although the transactional model offers fertile grounds for doing so.

The results just described are based upon leadership studies conducted in the private sector. However, similar findings generalize to the public sector as well. In a laboratory experiment conducted by Rice, Bender, and Vitters

(1980) at West Point, researchers found that male cadet followers, who held very traditional views regarding the rights and roles of women in society, tended to make less favorable judgments about the causes of successful leader performance in groups led by women than in groups led by men. The attitudes toward the roles of women is clearly an operational measure of sex-roles, and in the laboratory study it has a statistically significant interaction or relationship with the sex of the leader and follower performance.

The followers with traditional attitudes or conservative sex-roles indicated that the leader's hard work and the followers' cooperation played a less powerful role in groups with female leaders. Also, followers with traditional sex-role attitudes reported that luck was a stronger determinant of success for groups led by women. What we see coming into question is the transactional relationship or the transaction process where leader influence and follower compliance are contaminated by attitudes toward women's roles as measured by gender stereotypes and sex of the leader.

In addition to leader traits and behaviors, a third determinant in the approach to leadership involves the situational context in which the leaders and followers must function. The situational context for leadership includes factors such as tasks and resources of the group, the structure for roles, and the physical setting as well as the history of the group. The situational context, although well described using male subjects, has been only minimally addressed by researchers in the context of including women as leaders.

Most empirical studies of women as leaders in a situational context have been conducted with undergraduate subjects and, perhaps, graduate management students using surveys and laboratory studies. Often, the type of task used by laboratory researchers involved written descriptions of leaders rather than "real life" interactions. As a result, the findings of such laboratory studies have been questioned regarding their generalizablility to organizational life. Osborn and Vicars (1976) note that "artifical short-term laboratory studies tend to elicit subject responses based upon readily available stereotypes" (p. 447). Also, in the lab, women and men are randomly assigned to the role of leader. In the field, men and women self-select for leadership and/or are weeded out by others (Hollander & Yoder, 1980). Hence, female leaders in the field want the role of the leader and may be better prepared to fill it effectively.

Many would agree from an academic or scholastic perspective that more rigor is needed in assessing the outcomes of leadership involving women. However, few studies have actually used objective measures of performance despite their importance as a major index measure of leadership. On the other hand, field studies are very difficult to implement for a number of practical reasons. Indeed, one of the important limitations is the number of women in leadership roles in organizations or across organizations which can be matched with appropriate criteria. According to Kanter (1977), even when women are in some hierarchical positions, they are too often in leadership positions which are limited because they are tokens. Thus, influence in this case is minimal. Certainly, objective measures in actual work settings would be almost impossible to obtain for any large sample.

How Do You Rate on a Scale to Measure Sex-Role Attitudes?

This next section contains a sex-role inventory called the Attitudes Toward Women Scale (AWS), an instrument developed by Spence and Helmreich (1972; Spence, Helmreich, & Stapp, 1973). It contains statements which describe the roles, privileges, and rights that women ought to have in American society. Before reading any further, the reader may wish to complete the Attitudes Toward Women Scale given in Table 7.

The statements listed below describe attitudes toward the roles of women in society which different people have. There are no right or wrong answers, only opinions. You are asked to express your feeling about each statement by indicating whether you (A) agree strongly, (B) agree mildly, (C) disagree mildly, or (D) disagree strongly.

Scoring the AWS

Each person completing the questionnaire indicates his or her agreement with each statement on a four-point scale which ranges from "agree strongly" to " disagree strongly." The questions have a response range of 0 to 3, with the high score given to the end of each item indicating positive attitudes toward the role of women. Possible total scores (sums of the item scores) run from 0 to 45.

If a person's score on the AWS is high, he or she is classified as egalitarian, or open about the roles, privileges, and rights of women in society. If a person's score is low, he or she is classified as traditional or conservative regarding the roles and rights of women. A high AWS score is approximately 33 and above; low AWS scores are 27 and below. Often, median splits have been used to delineate traditional versus egalitarian attitudes. Spence and Helmreich (1978) have reported that they have validated expected differences between various groups. For example, they report that women score higher than men. Also, college students score higher than their same-sex parent. A more complete discussion of these differences is reported by Spence and Helmreich (1972). If you have just completed the AWS scale, you have a score in which you describe yourself as traditional or egalitarian. Later in chapters 3 and 4, you will see how similar scoring procedures were used to examine leadership in some situational context.

Recall from our earlier discussion in chapter 1 that a complete theory of leadership should explain: (a) the emergence of a leader; (b) the process that

Table 7
Attitudes Toward Women Scale

The statements listed below describe attitudes toward the roles of women in society which different people have. There are no right or wrong answers, only opinions. You are asked to express your feeling about each statement by indicating whether you (A) agree strongly, (B) agree mildly, (C) disagree mildly, or (D) disagree strongly.

1. Swearing and obscenity are more repulsive in the speech of a woman than a man.

A	B	C	D
Agree strongly	Agree mildly	Disagree mildly	Disagree strongly

2. Under modern economic conditions with women being active outside the home, men should share in household tasks such as washing dishes and doing the laundry.

A	B	C	D
Agree strongly	Agree mildly	Disagree mildly	Disagree strongly

3. It is insulting to women to have the "obey" clause remain in the marriage service.

A	B	C	D
Agree strongly	Agree mildly	Disagree mildly	Disagree strongly

4. A woman should be as free as a man to propose marriage.

A	B	C	D
Agree strongly	Agree mildly	Disagree mildly	Disagree strongly

5. Women should worry less about their rights and more about becoming good wives and mothers.

A	B	C	D
Agree strongly	Agree mildly	Disagree mildly	Disagree strongly

6. Women should assume their rightful place in business and all the professions along with men.

A	B	C	D
Agree strongly	Agree mildly	Disagree mildly	Disagree strongly

7. A woman should not expect to go to exactly the same places or to have quite the same freedom of action as a man.

A	B	C	D
Agree strongly	Agree mildly	Disagree mildly	Disagree strongly

8. It is ridiculous for a woman to run a locomotive and for a man to darn socks.

A	B	C	D
Agree strongly	Agree mildly	Disagree mildly	Disagree strongly

Table 7 (cont'd)

9. The intellectual leadership of a community should be largely in the hands of men.

A	B	C	D
Agree strongly	Agree mildly	Disagree mildly	Disagree strongly

10. Women should be given equal opportunity with men for apprenticeship in the various trades.

A	B	C	D
Agree strongly	Agree mildly	Disagree mildly	Disagree strongly

11. Women earning as much as their dates should bear equally the expense when they go out together.

A	B	C	D
Agree strongly	Agree mildly	Disagree mildly	Disagree strongly

12. Sons in a family should be given more encouragement to go to college than daughters.

A	B	C	D
Agree strongly	Agree mildly	Disagree mildly	Disagree strongly

13. In general, the father should have greater authority than the mother in the bringing up of children.

A	B	C	D
Agree strongly	Agree mildly	Disagree mildly	Disagree strongly

14. Economic and social freedom is worth far more to women than acceptance of the ideal of femininity which has been set up by men.

A	B	C	D
Agree strongly	Agree mildly	Disagree mildly	Disagree strongly

15. There are many jobs in which men should be given preference over women in being hired or promoted.

A	B	C	D
Agree strongly	Agree mildly	Disagree mildly	Disagree strongly

From *Masculinity and Femininity,* (pp. 237–239), by J. T. Spence and R. L. Helmreich, 1978, Austin, TX: University of Texas Press. Copyright © 1978 by J. T. Spence and R. L. Helmreich. Reprinted by permission.

leaders employ to maintain influence over followers; (c) the relation of the leader's attributes and style to group processes; and (d) the social context that is most supportive for leader traits and style to be effective (Stogdill, 1974). If we reexamine these criteria in light of two new traits—gender and sex, we may conclude that the concept of leadership as a personality characteristic again is oversimplified. Earlier studies do not imply that individual differences have nothing at all to do with leadership, but rather that the significance of individual variations must be evaluated in relation to the situation (Vroom, 1976). New evidence considering the effects of sex-roles or gender and biological sex indicates that the salience of trait theories needs to be reinvestigated as women hold increasing numbers of leadership positions.

As we look at leader behavior, it can be assessed in two ways: objective performance and subjective evaluation. The early Ohio State and Michigan studies during the 1950s and those that followed adopted a leader-style index based on scores reflecting task orientation or concern for people. Unlike early theorists studying leader style and behavior, Likert (1967), Blake and Mouton (1964), McGregor (1960), and others ascribe to a wide range of behavioral principles. They have the advantage of not dealing in any specific way with the complexities of situational differences and the impact of situations on leader behavior. But, according to Vroom (1976), the more broadly stated the principle the more likely it will be empirically vacuous and prescriptively useless. It is possible to state styles of leadership in such a way that they are truisms or are incapable of empirical refutation which elicit immediate acceptance by persons with drastically different leadership styles. To say that a leader should manage in such a way that followers at all levels feel really responsible for attainment of organizational goals or to say that the leader should exhibit concern for both task and subordinate welfare is not saying a great deal about what that leader should do in particular situations. Nor does such an approach guide leaders in concrete situations that they must face daily.

Objectively, women can be assessed as to whether they behave in a prescribed or functional manner in an organization. In order for the subjective perception of these behaviors to be accurate we need to control for sex-role or gender bias. By ascribing to a transactional approach which will focus on personal traits and how leaders behave in unique organizational settings, it is necessary to develop a set of concepts which is capable of dealing with differences in different situations and a parallel set of concepts capable of differentiating leaders and their styles. Such a theory which is arrived at by induction suggests that it becomes critical for a model to be validated by determining whether it will predict results other than those which entered into its formulation. This is important for leadership in the 1980s and in the decades to follow. Certainly, the leadership models and heuristics that have been ascribed to date are based upon those variables which were salient when leadership was studied. Today and in the foreseeable future, the importance of sex-roles and sex differences as they relate in a processual way will have a tremendous impact on leadership in the future.

In this chapter we introduced a number of factors necessary for a contemporary transactional approach of leadership which has utility for male and female leaders. These elements are based on some things gleaned from previous approaches that have been reviewed in the first chapter as well as the more general knowledge concerning human behavior, based upon the authors' personal studies of new elements influencing leadership processes in organizations. Next, we will introduce a framework of the leadership process to illustrate the approach.

CONCEPTUAL AND EMPIRICAL BASES OF LEADERSHIP

According to Vroom (1976), a framework designed to regulate, in some rational way, choices among leadership behaviors should be based upon sound empirical evidence concerning the likely consequences of styles. The more complete the empirical base of knowledge, the greater the certainty with which one can develop the theoretical framework, and the greater will be its usefulness. An aid in this analysis of existing evidence is to distinguish between the key elements that make up this framework.

The reader may recall that the main tenets of the transactional approach to leadership can be found in the work of Thibaut and Kelley (1959), Homans (1961), Jacobs (1971) and, more recently, Hollander (1978). Further, this conceptulization of leadership revolves around a reciprocal influence process in which each participant has the potential to exert influence. There are few distinctions between leaders and followers. Influence with others may be by providing a resource, fulfilling expectations, or by helping the group to achieve its goals.

Because transactional theory views leadership as a social-exchange process between leaders and those who are followers, both followers and leaders are seen as active participants in the leadership process. This dynamic exchange represents one of the distinctive aspects of this approach to leadership. In a general sense, leaders and followers are thought of as collaborators in the accomplishment of group goals.

Effective leadership is considered to be the initiation of an influence attempt and acceptance of this attempt by followers. Both the leader and the followers must feel mutually satisfied by the exchanges they make with one another. According to Hollander and Julian (1969), when leaders are effective they give something and get something in return. In exchange for the benefits followers receive from the leader, the leader receives greater influence, status, and esteem.

Thus, the leader's position, perceptions, resources relevent to accomplishment of the group's goals, and the followers (with their positions, perceptions, and relevant resources), considered together are important in determining the quality of the exchange and thereby leader and group effectiveness. The transactional approach to leadership also views the situational context in which the leader–member exchange process takes place as an important determinant of leader and group effectiveness.

Many variables which have received considerable attention include the source of the leader's authority; success/failure performance feedback; quantity and quality of participation in situations of emergent leadership; leader legitimacy and leader innovation (Hollander & Julian, 1969; Hollander, 1978; Bender, 1979). However, given the defined scope of leadership as a transactional process, it is unlikely that the exact nature of the effects of all relevant variables have been identified. Finally, the emergence of women as both leaders and followers will continue in almost all organizational settings. Thus, we believe that the influence of both sex-roles as operationally described by masculinity and femininity and sex-role attitudes should be added to contemporary models of transactional leadership. Many practicing managers may find themselves caught up in the confusion of melding sex-roles, gender attitudes, and sex differences. In the former case, leaders judge whether women "ought" to be performing in male-dominant positions. In the latter case, leaders ask if women "can" perform in masculine-dominated tasks.

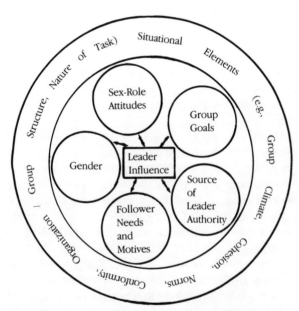

Figure 2.   Transactional Model of Leadership.

Judgments about how well women actually perform (sex differences) are clouded by beliefs and feelings about how women should perform. Our model separates the gender and sex differences. Please keep these distinctions in mind when we discuss research about the unique and joint influence of these elements on the leadership process.

A contemporary transactional model of leadership is described in Figure 2. Let us look more closely at each of the elements which are shown in a contemporary transactional model of leadership. Note that the factors which the leader can influence are not unidirectional, and hence, the bidirectional arrows. The process is reciprocal; these factors influence the leader, who, in turn, affects the effectiveness of the group.

Followers' Needs and Motives.   In any transactional process, followers play a crucial role in the leader's ability to exert influence. To the degree that followers perceive that the leader is able to facilitate their satisfaction of needs, they will be motivated to continue to allow the leader to exert influence. If they perceive that the leader's influence can no longer facilitate satisfaction of those needs, the leader's influence will decrease.

Source of Leader Authority.   There are many kinds of leaders who are either appointed, elected, or emergent. Within the type of appointment is the basis of formal power (legitimate, reward, coercive) and personal power (referent, expert). The leader's success in influencing followers is predicated on the source of authority and remains as long as followers are willing to comply with the authority.

Group Goals.   Clear identification and support of functional goals provide a focus and sense of direction for group activity. In consonance with follower motives, the leader's influence is directed toward attainment of group goals while satisfying followers' needs. It is not enough for the leader alone to define group goals. There must be shared beliefs whereby the followers accord the leader extra status, prestige, etc., as the group pursues goal attainment.

Sex-Roles.   Attitudes of followers have been an important influential factor to determine appropriate leadership behavior and style. In the foreseeable future, the emergence of women into less traditional roles questions the salience of sex-role attitudes in the leadership process. Ultimately, the response of subordinates to the leader determines how effective the leader will be. Therefore, follower compliance to leaders in nontraditional roles adds the new dimension to the leadership process. The issue is not, can the leader influence, but ought the leader exercise this influence?

Sex Differences. The need to conduct research on leader and follower sex as a factor in leadership is well established (Deaux, 1976b; Rice, Bender, & Vitters, 1980). The transactional process that occurs between a male leader and all-male followers differs from the influence between a male leader and a mixed group of followers, female leaders with female followers, etc. At the heart of this relationship is the assumption introduced by Graen (1976) that there is a unique vertical linkage between the leader and each follower. In other words, leader influence is not merely the sum or average of all follower responses to the leader's influence. The factor of biological sex adds additional attention to the leadership influence process.

Situational Elements. Every group develops a "personality" of its own. In a formal organization the environment or "climate" has some effect on group structure and policies to describe the nature of formal interactions between the leader and subordinates. Even in informal groups, situational elements such as group cohesion, norms, and conformity all exert an impact on the reciprocal-influence process between the leader and followers. Taken together, these factors affect the social-exchange process as well as the effectiveness of influence between the leader and those who are led.

Implications for Leaders

As can be seen in the defined scope of the transactional view of leadership, leader sex and sex-role attitudes are only two variables among many which can affect the exchange relationship between leaders and followers. The transactional view of leadership has evolved from nearly 70 years of leadership research, and it is still without a clear definition of interactive effects but for a small number of variables (Stogdill, 1974). In comparison, research on the effects of gender and sex-role attitudes is relatively new and has been conducted without the benefit of a conceptual model other than the one proposed here. As such, the discussion in this book of research findings and their applications for women as leaders is important, because these studies have considered those issues which are of concern in a contemporary perspective of transactional leadership. The issues addressed in these studies include: the effects of attitudes toward sex-roles and leadership; the effects of leader style and behavior of male and female leaders on group performance and followers' satisfaction; and the personality characteristics of women as leaders and the effects of situational variables on women as leaders. These are both highly complex and highly interactive, and in some cases, the results are not patterned in the same way for male and female leaders. What is needed is continued research along these lines, as well as research which focuses on leader sex with variables that have not been previously combined. Our transactional approach to leadership offers an opportunity for a more complete study of leadership.

SUMMARY

In this chapter we have described leadership as an influence process between the leader and the followers who accept and support this influence. We have discussed the leadership process as being transactional, involving a two-way influence in the relationship as well as reviewing several popular definitions of the term leadership. The transactional view is the most complete in its description of what takes place between followers and the leader. Not even the orthodox description of the leadership process is complete enough to stand alone. It is testimony to the state of the discipline to note that most of leadership theory and research has been conducted by men using male participants.

In looking to the changing values and roles of men and women in society during the 1980s, we see a shift in the rights, privileges, and roles of women in leadership. Therefore, sex-roles and biological sex are two new important factors which greatly affect the leader–follower reciprocal influence process. No conceptualization of these factors in any holistic sense has evolved in the scientific writings on leadership to date, yet these variables are of seminal importance to understanding the leadership processes in groups and organizations. Finally, we introduce an eclectic model of leadership, one which readily reorganizes the effects of sex-roles, sex, group goals, follower needs, and source of leader authority together. These variables operate in a unique manner in the context of situational environs of organizational climate or informal environments where group norms, cohesion, and conformity impact on the leader. In the next four chapters we will present research on the factors selected in the model and discuss the utility of the findings to theories of leadership and application of findings for practitioners.

Chapter 3

Personality and Situational Viewpoints

In chapter 1, we discussed various approaches to examine leadership. Historically, researchers began their study of leadership by searching for the personality characteristics of leaders that suited leaders for that position. Later researchers considered situational factors, while contemporary theorists propose an interactive influence. In two recent theories, the contingency model and transactional theory, situational factors combine with personal qualities of the leader to influence effective leadership. Research involving these theories will be discussed in chapter 4. In this chapter, we will look at recent research on personality and situational factors.[1] Although the interactive relationship between personality and situational variables should not be forgotten, the impact and implications of each are more clearly seen when viewed separately.

PROJECT ATHENA: PERSONALITY INVESTIGATIONS

The research presented here and in chapter 4 is part of a massive research effort at the U.S. Military Academy at West Point.[2] This research, appropriately

---

[1]Technical terminology and statistics have been kept to a minimum in the discussion of research in these two chapters. The only statistical test that could not be avoided is correlations. Correlations indicate the degree to which two variables are related and the nature of this relationship. Correlations range from -1.0 to $+1.0$ in value. Positive correlations indicate that the two variables are positively related—as one increases, so does the other. For example, height and weight are positively correlated. When one variable (e.g., altitude) increases as the other decreases (e.g., temperature), these variables are negatively correlated. A correlation of zero reveals that the variables in question are totally unrelated. The closer the value of the correlation is to one, the more strongly related are the variables. Correlations simply describe the degree to which two variables are related; they do not prove that one variable caused the other.

[2]Much of the data collected for this project is reported in four technical reports of the U.S. Military Academy. See Adams (1979, 1980), Vitters (1978), and Vitters and Kinzer (1977).

dubbed Project Athena, was sparked by the admission of 119 women cadets in 1976 to West Point. Project Athena is a longitudinal program which followed these men and women through their four years of training at the Academy and includes a look at subsequent classes as well. An extension of this work continues in the form of a postgraduation assessment of the first three coeducational classes from West Point. The male and female graduates provide an ideal group of leaders in the regular U.S. Army. Thus, we are able to substantiate leadership influence and processes in actual work settings. What follows is practical information useful to those who study leadership as well as those who are involved in its practice.

The training of leaders is the primary mission of the U.S. Military Academy. With the entry of women, the Academy was fertile ground for studying gender similarities and differences in leadership. Project Athena, a longitudinal study of the intergration of women into West Point, was designed to do just that. The research reviewed in the next two chapters focuses on men and women as both leaders and followers within a leadership setting. Although gender and sex-roles are the primary elements of these leadership research projects, other aspects of leadership will be examined.

The research described here was conducted in a military setting. This has several advantages. First, the findings of all of these studies are directly comparable to one another. Second, the long-term nature of the project permitted a longitudinal look at the leadership process which is not afforded by short-term studies. In other words, we were able to identify patterns of relationships with the same cohesive, functioning groups over several years. The third advantage of this study is the richness of the data. Project Athena comprises experimental, laboratory studies, surveys, field studies, observations, and interviews. This allows us to triangulate our findings, using several independent methodologies simultaneously.

The one obvious question both the theorist and practitioner may ask concerns the generalizability of findings gleaned within the military setting to other organizational settings. However, even this possibility need not be overly worrisome. The research that has been done within Project Athena is firmly rooted within the theoretical perspectives reviewed in chapter 1. The guidance of these perspectives, which themselves have been developed with both military and civilian inputs, has pervaded each research project, thus enhancing the generalizability of each project to other times, places, and participants.

The Leader's Personality

Intelligence: A Personality Trait. Fiedler and contingency theorists have long been interested in the relationship between the intelligence of group members and the effectiveness of group task performance. Implicit in this concern has been the common-sense notion that groups with more intelligent leaders (and/or followers) perform more effectively on most assigned group tasks than groups with less intelligent leaders (and/or followers). However, much small-group research has shown that this positive relationship between intelligence and group task performance was not always found in empirical studies (Calvin, Hoffman, & Harden, 1957). Fiedler and his associates have tried to identify the conditions under which this positive relationship does and does not hold.

In the first effort to integrate such results, Fiedler and Meuwese (1963) examined the relationship between leaders' intelligence and group performance in a variety of field and laboratory settings. They concluded that the correlation between leaders' intelligence and group performance was substantial only among groups with high cohesiveness.

Several years later, Blades and Fiedler (1973) considered leaders' characteristics that moderated the relationship between followers' intelligence and group performance. With several samples of military persons, they found positive and significant correlations between average followers' intelligence and group task performance among groups with relationship-oriented (high LPC—Least Preferred Co-worker) leaders. Among groups with task-oriented (low LPC) leaders, the relationship essentially was zero.

More recently, Fiedler and Leister (1977) expanded their analyses of the relationship between leaders' intelligence and group performance. They presented a theoretical model identifying factors that can "screen" out the impact of leaders' intelligence on group performance. These screen variables interfere with the influence that leaders' intelligence would normally have on group performance. Fiedler and Leister (1977) presented empirical findings from several different research settings that support the presence of these screen variables.

For example, Fiedler and Leister identified a stressful relationship with one's boss as one such screen variable. When there was little stress with the boss, the intelligence of U.S. Army infantry squad leaders was positively correlated with ratings of effective performance in the military. In contrast, no relationship between intelligence and performance was found for leaders working under stressful conditions. The overall correlation of intelligence and performance would be insignificant; however, when the researcher identified the appropriate screen variable, in this case stress, a significant relationship between intelligence and performance was uncovered.

Project Athena provided another opportunity to test the screen hypothesis because the data set included:

1. a general measure of both leaders' and followers' intelligence (American College Test (ACT) and/or Scholastic Aptitude Test (SAT) scores);

2. objective measures of group performance from 72 groups of three men, half led by a male cadet, half by a female cadet, on two tasks (structured: making a scale drawing of a building; unstructured: writing a proposal to increase enlistment rates); and
3. a host of personality and demographic variables that were analyzed as potential screen variables (Adams, Prince, Yoder, & Rice, 1981; Yoder, Rice, & Adams, 1979).

Two of these potential screen factors were the leader's sex and the followers' sex-role attitudes.[3] We hypothesized that the correlation between leaders' and followers' intelligence and group performance would be weaker in groups with female leaders than in groups with male leaders. As noted previously, in chapter 1, much research indicates that the leadership role is essentially a masculine one. Thus, the energy devoted to such maintenance issues may dilute the impact of intellectual resources of both female leaders and their followers. We also hypothesized, based on a similar rationale, that the screen effect would be especially strong for groups composed of female leaders and followers with traditional attitudes toward female and male sex-roles.

The findings indicate that leaders' intelligence was related to group performance on the structured drawing task, but only for male leaders of groups with traditional sex-role attitudes. In other words, groups holding traditional attitudes about sex-roles performed well on the drawing task when they were led by intelligent male leaders. The performance of similar groups was low with a less intelligent male leader. Furthermore, the higher the intelligence of male leaders of followers with traditional attitudes, the more highly these leaders rated their importance to the group and the cooperation of group members. These intelligent leaders also showed more consideration toward group members and initiated structure on the task. Thus, the intelligent, traditional male leader of followers with traditional attitudes felt important and helped, and, in turn, exhibited consideration toward, and initiated structure for, these supportive, high-performing followers. Leaders' intelligence and group performance are related to some degree, but only through the screen variables of leaders' gender and followers' sex-role attitudes.

The intelligence of female leaders was unrelated to performance on both tasks, even when the screen variables were considered. However, the intelligence of the overall group was related to drawing performance. More intelligent groups with egalitarian sex-role attitudes performed better on the drawing task when led by a woman than when led by a man.

None of the other individual personality variables, such as locus of con-

---

[3]Sex-role attitudes were measured by responses to Spence and Helmreich's (1972) Attitudes toward Women Scale (AWS) (Yoder, Rice, Adams, Priest, & Prince, 1982).

trol, self-concept, and LPC, proved to be significant screen variables.[4] The group's attitudes toward sex-roles and the leader's sex were interesting and interactive screen variables. Since the subjects were cadets in the first class at West Point to include women, it is reasonable to find that the leader's sex and attitudes toward sex-roles were salient screen variables. It is conceivable that notions involving men's and women's roles were foremost in the minds of most cadets, male and female, at that time.

The fact that screen effects were found for performance on only the structured drawing task is noteworthy. The key may lie in the operational definition of intelligence. In the present study, intelligence was defined as scholastic aptitude, which measures academic skills that may be most relevant to a structured task. Measures of leaders' creativity, for example, may be more relevant to a group's performance on an unstructured task requiring originality.

The most interesting outcome of these analyses concerns the fact that followers' attitudes and leader's sex interact as significant screen variables. There is no simple effect of the leader's sex. Instead, the leader's intelligence and group performance are related only under certain conditions involving both the followers' and the leader's characteristics. This supports the notion that leadership involves a transactional process between the leader and followers (Hollander, 1978).

When the leader is male and intelligent, group performance on a structured task is maximized when the followers hold traditional sex-role attitudes. More intelligent groups perform well on the structured task when the followers are supportive of an egalitarian role for women and men and the leader is a woman. It may be useful for project directors to take into account the intelligence and gender of a leader as well as the attitudes of followers when assigning a leader to his or her role.

Other Personality Characteristics

As already mentioned, Project Athena is filled with personality measures. However, as we saw in chapter 1, research on the relationship between personality characteristics of leaders and leadership behavior was not encouraging. We decided to take a global look at these variables to see which, if any, were related to group performance on the same two tasks: drawing and drafting a proposal (Yoder, Rice, Adams, Prince, & Hicks, 1979).

---

[4]Locus of control refers to the degree to which an individual believes life events are internally or externally caused (Rotter, 1966). Self-concept was measured by the Tennessee Self-Concept Scale (TSCS) and LPC by Fiedler's Least Preferred Coworker Scale (see chap. 1). Other personality variables studied were masculinity and femininity (Personal Attributes Questionnaire; Spence, Helmreich, & Stapp, 1974) and a rating of leadership behavior used at West Point (Priest, 1975).

In this study, nine unrelated personality variables were identified: leadership ability, sex-role attitudes, LPC, male and female valued qualities, math and verbal SAT scores, locus of control, and self-concept.[5] We found that male leaders who rated themselves as low in feminine qualitites led groups that performed well on the unstructured task. More task-oriented (low LPC) female leaders led successful groups in the same task. No personality correlates were found for the structured task.

The results of our efforts to predict group task performance on the basis of leaders' personality characteristics were quite consistent with the generally negative results of previous research along these lines. Even with the substantial number of variables available in the Project Athena data set, we were not able to identify individual personality characteristics of the leader or combinations of such characteristics with much ability to predict task performance by the group. These rather negative conclusions hold for analyses of the entire sample as well as for separate analyses on male and female leaders.

The only exception to these negative findings concerns the degree to which leaders conform to a masculine stereotype. Two significant correlates of performance on the proposal task suggest that more stereotypically masculine leaders have more effective groups. When women are task-oriented (a masculine ascribed trait) and men score low in characteristics stereotypically associated with femininity, their groups perform better on an ambiguous, unstructured task. With a clear task to perform, ambiguities surrounding the appropriateness of the actual leader for the stereotypic masculine leadership role do not seem to influence group performance. Again, this suggests the importance of the transaction between leaders and followers and shifts our focus from personality characteristics alone toward roles and the way these influence leadership behavior.

Conclusion

The personality characteristics of the leader do not predict group performance at West Point. There is some evidence that the intelligence of the leader influences group performance when both the role of the leader is filled by a man and group members hold traditional sex-role attitudes. The more in keeping with sex-role stereotypes of leadership both male and female leaders are, the more effective these leaders seem to be. Two conclusions can be drawn from these findings: (a) role expectations about the

---

[5]These nine factors were the result of factor analyzing a set of 25 personality measures. A varimax rotation assured us that these factors indeed were orthogonal. Leadership ability is a composite of ratings by each cadet's peers, upper-class cadet squad leaders, and officers recorded at the end of each of their first two semesters at the Academy (see fn. 4 for additional references).

leader are more important in predicting group performance than personality characteristics; and (b) evidence is mounting in support of a transactional exchange between leaders and followers.

PROJECT ATHENA: ORGANIZATIONAL INFLUENCES AND THE SITUATION

We noted earlier that leadership is influenced by the social context in which it occurs. The situation affects leadership on three interrelated levels: (a) interpersonal, (b) organizational, and (c) societal. Roles reflect the interpersonal nature of leadership in that they emphasize the complementarity of leader's and followers' roles. Our discussion of situational influences on leadership behavior will begin by examining leadership as a role.

Next to be considered will be the organizational level and the way that its policies, such as those that create the sex composition of the group and, in some cases, tokenism, influence leadership. Finally, the societal impact on leadership will be examined. Authoritarian, democratic, and laissez-faire leaders may be regarded differently by followers from Western, Asian, and Latin American societies (Robertson, 1977). These differential expectations in turn may affect the transactional processes of leadership.

Role Influences

Two types of leadership roles were identified by Bales and Slater (1955): (a) instrumental and (b) socioemotional or expressive. Persons filling the instrumental role focus on the tasks to be accomplished; on the other hand, socioemotional leaders concentrate on the satisfaction and morale of group members. Roles are created by the group to meet group needs. In contrast, traits and leaders' styles are personal factors residing within leaders which are brought by them to the group. Therefore, in order to study roles, the focus will be on followers' *perceptions* of leaders' behavior. As will be seen, leaders are evaluated by followers according to how well the leaders fill the roles created by the group.

Leaders are expected to be men. The masculine role overlaps to a large extent with that of middle manager, whereas the feminine role does not (Schein, 1973). Within Project Athena, we found that followers held different beliefs about male and female leaders. Subordinates believed that female leaders had more concern for the welfare of the troops (consideration). There were no difference in descriptions of initiation of structure by female and male platoon leaders (Adams & Hicks, 1978).

The impact of others' expectations about the leader's role is illustrated in a study conducted by Adams and Hicks (1981). During the summer before their second year of training at West Point, all cadets participate in Cadet Field

Training (CFT) where they are introduced to the combat arms and combat support branches of the U.S. Army, e.g., Armor, Infantry, Engineering, Field Artillery, Air Defense Artillery, and Signal. CFT is physically demanding, stressing physical effort and endurance. Long hours, marches, calisthenics, and field rations supply some of the daily fare of CFT to simulate the conditions of the real Army.

One important goal of CFT is to develop the leadership skills of the participating cadets. Therefore, cadets are assigned to temporary leadership positions during the course of training. For example, a cadet might serve as squad leader or as a section chief or platoon sergeant for a temporary period in training, and then, at the end of the same day, the cadet would return to the role of squad member. Thus, there is a continuous rotation of leadership roles.

At several points during the course of training, the performance of cadets at CFT is formally evaluated by either upper-class West Point cadets or by the regular U.S. Army officers who supervise cadet training (i.e., tactical officers). A cadet may be a squad member, a leader, or in a supervisory staff role at the time of these evaluations. Typical supervisory positions include transportation sergeant, supply sergeant, training sergeant, and so on. Such positions carry considerable responsibility but are outside the direct line of command and have limited authority when compared to line leader roles, such as assistant squad leader, squad leader, or platoon leader.

Cadets' performance appraisal ratings, developed and regularly collected under institutional authority, served as the data analyzed for the study by Adams and Hicks (1981). The major objective of these analyses was to compare the ratings given to male and female cadets as they performed temporary military training exercises in each of three roles: squad member, formal leader, and supervisor.

Let us stop and examine these three roles within this social context which emphasizes physical prowess. Physical superiority generally is granted to men, both stereotypically and at the Academy in actuality, a point noted by continual references to the proven superior upper-body strength of men (Adams, 1979). Hence, the role of leader, regarded as masculine in general, is even more appropriate for men within this context which stresses physical ability. Aspects of the managerial role, such as forcefulness and directing others, also are generally attributed to men, whereas other aspects of this role, such as adjusting to new situations, may be considered sex-role neutral. Finally, the role of follower or squad member is neutral, that is, equally appropriate for both women and men.

The purpose of our analysis is to examine how others regard the same men and women filling each of these three roles. Performance appraisals, which are a composite of ratings from tactical officers and more senior cadets, served as our measure of other people's perceptions. Are these perceptions related to what might be expected of women and men filling these three roles? If so, we would expect performance appraisals to be different for men and women who are squad leaders and similar when they fill the sex-role neutral position of squad member.

This is precisely what Adams and Hicks (1981) found. The smallest difference between the ratings of female and male cadets was found when they were members of a squad. On the six measures of performance recorded, there were no significant differences among male and female squad members. As administrative managers, there were no sex differences for three of these six variables (capacity for increased responsibility; adjusting to new situations; and support to supervisors and subordinates). The remaining three variables yielded significantly higher ratings for male cadets in administrative roles (organizing and directing the efforts of others; initiative, forcefulness, and aggressiveness; and overall performance of duties). Those aspects of the administrative role that are regarded as masculine (not too surprisingly) are evaluated more positively for men.

When the role, squad leader, is most appropriately masculine, men are rated significantly higher on five of the six scales. The only rating on which there is no sex difference is on evaluations of the squad leader's support of superiors and subordinates (consideration). Given that consideration is more readily granted to female leaders, then this must make up for the debilitating effects of this masculine role for the women cadets.

Although other explanations for these findings are possible, this explanation is consistent with all the data and is parsimonious. Roles are what people expect of others. When leaders do not "fit" their roles, this negatively affects others' evaluations of the leaders' performance. We saw this same process in chapter 1 when we discussed fear of success. As Cherry and Deaux (1978) discovered, when a role is sex-role inappropriate, people degrade others who play those roles. Subjects wrote demeaning stories of Anne in medical school and John in nursing school. Similar arguments regarding role compatibility seem to underlie later analyses involving these same women after their graduation in their roles as U.S. Army officers (see Yoder & Adams, 1984). Could the evaluators in the study by Adams and Hicks unintentionally be biased by their expectations? As we have seen, the more sex-role inappropriate the role one plays, the more negatively evaluated that person will be.

Organizational Influences

The type of leadership that is exhibited and that is effective is dependent upon the characteristics of the organization in which this leadership occurs. For example, organizational goals influence leadership. It seems reasonable to suggest that task completion is more important to profit-seeking organizations, whereas consideration may be at a premium in volunteer groups. The reward contingencies and opportunities for advancement within an organization also may affect leadership. If individual performance is rewarded and used as the basis for promotion, those who rise to positions of leadership will be best equipped to compete with others in their field. On the other hand, if group performance is stressed, leaders will be those who effectively coordinate cooperative ventures. If an organization, such as the military, is beaureaucratic and hierarchical, leadership will involve strong position power, and followers will be expected to be submissive and disciplined. In structurally flatter organizations, other types of power, such as informational and expert power, will define effective leadership.

In her influential book *Men and Women of the Corporation,* Kanter (1977) showed that the composition of work groups can influence leadership. If a group is formed so that one subgroup, such as women, compose less than 15% of the entire group, this aspect of organizational membership can limit the performances of these underrepresented group members, called tokens by Kanter. Since we replicated some of Kanter's work in Project Athena, let us turn to our work on tokenism (Yoder, Adams, & Prince, 1983; Yoder, Adams, Grove, & Priest, in press).

Tokenism and Leadership

Tokenism is characterized by three features: (a) tokens compose less than 15% of the entire group (Kanter, 1977); (b) the dominant group was pressured by outside forces to share desirable commodities with the token group (Laws, 1975); and (c) the quantity and quality of the mobility of tokens are restricted (Laws, 1975). By this third factor, Laws means that the number of tokens to be admitted is limited (quantity) and that the system must not be changed to accommodate this new group, even though the system itself had been created without considering this token group (quality).

By this definition, the first women to enter the U.S. Military Academy at West Point in 1976 clearly were tokens. They were admitted in response to a Congressional mandate; these positions, by definition, had been exclusively male; and a West Point commission certainly proves advantageous for any Army officer pursuing advancement (Ellis & Moore, 1974). Furthermore, the equal opportunity goal for the admission of women is to seek a proportion of women cadets from 10 to 15% (Adams, 1979), and the Congressional mandate was clear in emphasizing that only those changes necessitated by physiological differences between men and women would be permitted (Defense Appropriations Authorization Act of 1976). Women cadets at West Point, as well as female managers studied by Kanter (1977) and college professors (Laws, 1975), meet these criteria for token status.[6]

---

[6]Recent research suggests that tokenism also involves the influence of societal sex-role stereotypes so that the negative consequences of numerical underrepresentation accrue only to women (Yoder & Sinnett, 1984).

The Price of a Token.   According to Kanter (1977), tokens are (a) visible, (b) contrasted, and (c) assimilated. *Visibility* occurs simply because the token is novel in a perceptual field of dominants. Visibility is a constant, obvious phenomenon. Even military uniforms do not completely integrate women into a company at West Point; a casual observer easily can identify women cadets as they march by in a parade. Visibility produces performance pressures for the tokens because their every move is noticed and easily recalled. Additionally, the natural visibility of tokens absorbs dominants into the perceptual ground, making dominants fearful that tokens may possess a competitive edge.

No one can deny that the admission of women into West Point received a great deal of news notoriety. Photographers were repeatedly singling out women for pictures; reporters were seeking women for personal interviews, and military VIPs always were close by as obtrusive observers to this change to West Point tradition. For example, during summer training and throughout the academic year, it was a common sight for the dominants to observe some high-ranking official or a media representative talking to a token about her early experiences or adjustment. But, as Kanter showed, even good press can be bad press when it emphasizes the visibility of tokens. This visibility, in turn, can lead to fears in dominants and performance pressures for the tokens.

The 1980 graduation of the first class of women brought female cadets back into the limelight. Many dominants became critical of the fact that more than 200 news personnel had applied for press passes to cover the first coed graduation. The common theme among male cadets became, "It's our graduation too." It is likely that the value of graduation ceremonies, a once-in-a-lifetime event, increased for male cadets, since they were indistinctive members of the dominant group (Fromkin, 1970). This, in turn, may have enhanced the intrusiveness for the men of the attention paid to women. Resentment among dominants was an inescapable byproduct of the notoriety of the successful female cadets.

This concern among dominant male cadets was evident at other times, most notably when competition existed for scarce, lucrative resources. Male cadets in the Class of 1980 (the first class with women cadets) expressed fears that women would receive first-choice assignments at the expense of men in troop leader training (summer exercises before the junior year designed to provide realistic leadership experiences). This fear also expressed itself within the military development system, a series of ratings of each cadet's leadership effectiveness which includes ratings from tactical officers and the cadre of upper-class cadets. For two consecutive years, women as a group received the lowest ratings from the members of the class immediately senior to their own (Adams, 1979), that is, from raters closest to the women competitively.

Of the five areas of cadet development (intellectual, military, moral/

ethical, physical, and social), the physical ability of cadets figures substantially into their success at West Point (Rice, Yoder, Adams, Priest, & Prince, 1984). It is in this area that sex differences were most pronounced and that West Point was given the leeway by the law to make accommodating changes. It was also in this area that women felt the strongest performance pressures and that institutional changes were most striking.

There is ample evidence that women in the first class felt pressured to perform well. For example, during Cadet Basic Training women reported feeling more stressed than did men. By the end of the 2-month initiation period, 16% of the women and 10% of the men left the Academy. Women entering in 1976 pushed themselves by ignoring physical maladies. These women missed physical training on a medical excuse half as often as later classes of women. As one tactical officer commented, "The women who fall out [of runs] really try hard to earn peer acceptance. They run on their own in their free time in the evening, but the daily training demands are so great on the body that these women are only continuing to tear down rather than build up their stamina" (Adams, 1979, p. 132).

Based on several studies, senior Academy officials adopted a policy of equivalent training in some physical tasks for women and men. These studies provided empirical evidence to describe anthropometric differences between women and men. However, these modifications in the physical education program were accepted critically by some male cadets as evidence that the admission of women resulted in lower standards. During interviews with officers at the various training sites, one officer indicated that he no longer wore his West Point class ring because he wanted to symbolize his rejection of the "new" Academy. A recurrent pattern in these interviews was for Academy personnel to equate substitutions, modifications, and deletions of physical activities with "lowered standards."

Like visibility, the *contrast* effect also results from the perceptual differences between tokens and dominants, but the emphasis here is on the difference itself. Individual dominants are unique, as are individual tokens, but the within-group differences fade in comparison with between-group contrasts. These group differences, or contrasts, generate uncertainties among dominants about how to act toward tokens. Every institution has its own norms which are communicated through informal, social networks. Tokens who do not fit into this network are isolated; thus, they lose an important source of information and interpersonal gratification. This especially is true at the Academy where an informal information network passes on hints about shortcuts for polishing shoes, making bunk beds, preparing for inspections, and cleaning rifles. On a more serious level, cadets conduct their own honor boards and can bring charges against others for suspected honor code violations.

It is cadets' concerns about dating that best reflected the effects of contrast. The social interaction of men and women at the Academy created uncertainties for the dominant men that did not exist before the admission of women. In response to a survey, some cadets defined dating as seeing a male and female cadet together on multiple occasions, and they regarded mere association as evidence of favoritism. This broad interpretation of the social interaction of women and men served to isolate women. Many dating couples were verbally and nonverbally harassed. This fear of favoritism was compounded by the fact that peers' and upper-class cadets' ratings contributed to each cadet's leadership evaluation. The result was an atmosphere in which women were defensive and wary of peer interactions that otherwise would have been professionally and personally gratifying.

Senior officials at the Academy have initiated several interventions designed to reduce the uncertainties of dominants about how to act toward tokens. For example, educational and training seminars and workshops have been conducted with dominant members in leadership roles. The focus of these activities has been on learning how to cope with the dynamics of mixed-sex units. Dating and fraternization (improper senior–subordinate relationships) policies were revised to provide clearer guidelines about appropriate and inappropriate behaviors.

Finally, the uncertainties of dominants as to how to act toward different tokens can be reduced readily by the use of stereotypes. Dominants may begin to treat tokens as generalized others, a process called *assimilation*. From the perspective of the token, assimilation creates role encapsulation. Paradoxically, the token, although clearly visible as an unique group member, loses some of his or her individuality and simply becomes a member of a stereotyped group who is expected by others to act (and succeed or fail) in stereotypic ways.

The stereotype that women are physically subordinate to men encouraged men simultaneously to protect women and to fear the preferential treatment of women and lowering of the Academy's standards. It is the protection of female cadets that most clearly demonstrates the assimilation of individual cadets into the stereotypical helpless role of women. During the summer training at Camp Buckner (CFT) where teams of sophomore cadets were required to assemble a temporary bridge, women were given less strenuous roles by their male peers and were physically relieved of heavy burdens. Specifically, interviews indicated that women of small stature and those who did not possess a "command voice" were most frequently the targets of stereotyping—and were assigned to less strenuous roles by team leaders.

Cadet women were encapsulated in their feminine role at other times as well. Before their third academic year (troop leader training), all cadets fill field assignments to give them hands-on leadership experience in the regular Army. Ratings of men and women cadets in their leadership roles showed some interesting sex differences. Women were described more favorably in their ability to communicate and work with seniors, peers, and subordinates (consideration). Raters described the primary strength of male cadets as initiative and assertiveness; women cadets were seen as working well with subordinates. Furthermore, when counselors were asked how each cadet could best use his or her energy to optimize self-development prior to commissioning, men were advised to seek more leadership experience, whereas women were told to develop their staff skills more fully (Adams, 1979). Again, women are placed in the nurturant, considerate feminine role which, unlike the masculine role, does not overlap with the more general role of leader. So, although both women and men are role-encapsulated, the role of the token is not favored by the dominant group which has set the standards of effectiveness and promotion.

Implications of Tokenism. Tokenism has several potential implications for leadership. First, since the token is plagued by constant visibility and the resultant performance pressures, will this token seek the limelight of the leadership position? Second, will the token who does seek leadership harbor greater resentments among colleagues because of the fears dominants already have about the apparent competitive edge of the visible token? Will these dominants then be less supportive of the leadership attempts of token members? Moreover, will the uncertainties of dominants toward contrasted, different tokens make tokens less desirable as both leaders and followers? Will dominants ask: How do I treat a token leader? (Should I take orders from her? How should I behave? Should I ask her out? What should I do with token followers? Can she keep up with the others? What if she cries?) Finally, will role encapsulation limit the flexibility of leaders? Will it affect ratings of their effectiveness?

These are just some of the questions researchers and policy makers may ask about the impact of tokenism on leadership. Although the data of Project Athena substantiated our notions that tokenism occurs at the Academy (as well as in business and academia), we did not as yet study leadership within the research paradigm of tokenism. Although the empirical answers to the above questions are yet to be generated, some intuitive answers may come to mind for the practitioner reading this segment. At least it is important to be aware of the impact that tokenism, as well as other organizational dynamics, may have on leadership processes.

Societal Influences on Leadership

At the societal level, leadership is viewed within a broad social, political, and economic order. In his classic book, Weber (1947), a sociologist, describes three pure types of legitimate authority (societal leadership). The claims of these leaders to legitimacy are based on: (a) rational grounds–legal authority; (b) traditional grounds–traditional authority, or (c) charismatic grounds–charismatic authority.

Legal authority is based within an impersonal, legally established, bureaucratic order. Authority rests within a position (position power) and not within the person filling that position. The power of the position is legally defined and granted. Legality, in turn, is defined by the acceptance of both the leader and followers of mutually interdependent ideas, for example, shared perceptions of what is rational or expedient.

Traditional authority demands obedience to the person who is the leader. The legitimacy of this person to demand obedience is bound in tradition. The personal authority of the leader and his or her claim to power is based in the sanctity of what has been handed down from the past. Obedience is not owed to exact rules but rather to the person tradition has chosen for the position of authority. Commands are legitimate because they conform to traditional dictates, and/or they reflect the chief's free personal decision.

Finally, charismatic authority rests in the exceptional characteristics of a given leader. This leader is obeyed by virtue of the personal trust followers hold. This leader rises to power because followers and the leader share the perception that a person who is charismatically endowed is duty-bound to accept leadership. Continuance as leader is dependent upon the constant exhibition of exemplary powers. The shared bond of the leader with followers is emotional.

Weber (1947) regards these three bases of legitimate authority as pure forms which are conceptually distant. However, real-life leadership is some combination of these factors. For example, Ronald Reagan fills the office of the U.S. Presidency and his authority is primarily legal. However, through his ability to appeal to the American people by exploiting his facility with the media, especially television, Reagan lays claim to some charismatic qualities as well.

Weber relates these grounds for legitimate authority to the economic order. Capitalism and socialism rest firmly on rational grounds, developing bureaucracies to administer to societal needs. Patrimonialism (inherited authority) is an example of traditional authority; the economic order reflects the monopoly of the leader over resources. Finally, charismatic leadership in its pure form is anti-economic. As charismatic leadership becomes routinized, it gathers some of the characteristics, and hence economic interests, of the other types of authority. For example, the originally charismatic fiefdom of feudalism was converted to patrimony by the appointment of successors within the charismatic leader's bloodline.

Sociologists offer us a broader view of leadership and its societal implications. Here, we are studying leadership within only one society and that society affects the leadership patterns which are exhibited and which are effective. For example, the emphasis on participative management in industrial and organizational psychology (e.g., Likert, 1967) and democratic styles of leadership (Lewin, Lippit, & White, 1939) reflect our economic and political biases, although other possibilities for leadership exist.

Conclusion

The situational influences on leadership are complex, evolving from the interrelationship of interpersonal, organizational, and societal aspect of the social context. These aspects of the situation do not operate in isolation, but rather they tend to be consistent with each other. For example, within a capitalist society, authority may be legally grounded, organizations may value productivity and profits, and the leader's role, in turn, may incorporate expectations regarding task-directiveness, decisiveness, and initiation of structure. Each aspect of the situation supports as well as reflects the others.

UTILITY AND IMPLICATIONS

Although an understanding of the situation helps explain and predict some leadership behaviors, it does not complete the entire picture of leadership. For example, knowing the leader's sex and interpersonal role definitions of what constitutes appropriate in-role behavior can help us understand some of the gender differences we have seen. However, as both Kanter (1977) and Bartol (1978) argue, individual differences in leadership style may be more predictive of effective leadership than gender per se. We offered this tenet in chapter 2 and some empirical evidence in chapter 3 supports this position. The key may be to examine the interaction of leader's characteristics with situational factors, including the characteristics of followers. It is to research dealing with this last idea that we will turn our attention in chapter 4.

Implications for Researchers and Practitioners

Before examining the interactive views of leadership, let us consider the implications of the research reviewed here for both future researchers and practitioners.

For Researchers.   Several ideas for future research can be extracted from the preceding review. First, both personality studies suggest that the characteristics of the task determine what characteristics of the leader are most important. Once the screen variables were removed, intelligence was related to group performance, only on the structured task. Concerns about role ambiguity and the sex-typing of leaders' behavior surfaced only for the unstructured task. When the demands of the task are unclear, sex-role ambiguities may be aggravated. As Hollander and Yoder (1980) suggest in their review of the literature on sex similarities and differences in leadership, further exploration of the impact of task characteristics on leadership behavior is warranted.

Second, both the personality and situational studies illustrate the importance of leaders' and followers' role expectations on the transactional leadership dynamic. Future studies should not focus solely on gender as a predictor of leadership, but rather they should combine leaders' sex types with the group's expectations regarding the appropriateness of the leadership role for women and men.

Osborn and Vicars (1976) suggest that research conducted in short-term laboratory experiments artificially exaggerates sex-role stereotypes, producing artifactual sex differences in leadership behavior. On the other hand, an examination of research in the field shows few sex differences, because the interaction of leaders with followers over time reduces the impact of simple sex-role expectations. The analyses presented here, which were conducted in both the lab and the field, do not support this interpretation as far as role expectations and their impact on followers' perceptions of leadership is concerned. This may be because issues concerning sex-roles were so salient in the field of a newly integrated Academy. Furthermore, these sex differences may apply only to those circumstances related to role expectations and not to other aspects of leadership, such as leaders' effectiveness.

Finally, researchers are encouraged to take a situation-centered, rather than a person-centered, view of leadership (Riger & Galligan, 1980). To examine leaders' sex per se is to look for person-centered explanations: It assumes that there is something within men and women themselves that creates gender differences in leadership. It is probably more enlightening to look for those qualities of the situation, such as followers' role expectations and task characteristics, that combine with gender to produce a specific configuration of leadership.

For Practitioners.   Leaders are not born; they are made and maintained by the followers who support them. One potential avenue for enhancing leadership potential is to create situations favorable to positive leadership. The focus here will be on designing situations to create both positive leadership and followership.

One potential debilitating organizational constraint on the exhibition of leadership is the existence of tokenism. The longitudinal nature and controlled environment of Project Athena have given us some insights into how to alter the situation to reduce tokenism. Although tokenism has not been fully eradicated from the Academy, it has been reduced in the first four years that the organization was coeducational. Plans to continue in this direction are still being formulated and implemented. The progress that has been achieved thus far can be attributed to three agents: the institution, the dominant group, and individual tokens (Yoder et al., 1980).

Institutional Policies. The institutional supports for reducing the token status of women cadets fall into three categories: (a) increased numbers over time, (b) sustained commitment to the success of women, and (c) a reassessment of training goals. Kanter (1977) suggests that increasing the number of outgroup members in an organization will reduce tokenism. The female cadets of 1976 composed less than 2% of the entire Corps; with new coeducational classes entering the Academy every year, these pioneer women at the time of their graduation made up 8% of the Corps.

As the number of women at West Point increased, some problems of the first class disappeared. Later classes of women were willing to admit physical illness or injury. Attrition rates for women leveled off and are more comparable to the percentages of men leaving each class. As women entered the ranks of upper-class cadets, they became the members of the cadet chain of command who lead and evaluate under-class cadets. These upper-class women, as well as new female tactical officers and female faculty members (civilian and military) served as role models (Darley, 1976). Simply put, time is an ally of change.

Although the passage of time has helped soothe the impact of change at West Point, it clearly is not a sufficient solution. In the course of many interviews conducted during the summer training sessions in 1980, some cadets and officers alike still voiced doubts about the admission of women. But the bottom line in all these conversations is that the orders are clear and unwavering: Women are to be integrated in the Corps of Cadets. "Women are coming to West Point," wrote the former Superintendent in 1975. "We have our orders, and it is our responsibility to implement them to the best of our ability" (Vitters & Kinzer, 1977). This philosophy has persisted at West Point; officially, the debate about the appropriateness of cadet women ended in 1975. In his annual Fall address to the staff and faculty in 1978, the Superintendent stated that women are at West Point to stay. He cemented his position by offering to arrange for the reassignment of any staff member who felt that he or she could not support women at the Academy. Unwavering institutional support has contributed to the successes of the token group (Pettigrew, 1961).

The final institutional support involves a reassessment of training goals. Recognizing the impact of physical ability on performance ratings and peer acceptance, a series of studies was conducted, and changes were made in the training schedules of freshmen and sophomore cadets. Most changes centered around differential upper-body strength. Although the resultant cries by some Academy personnel was that standards had been lowered, an underlying bias has emerged: Each change was made to reduce the failures of female cadets and not to exploit the valuable contributions women have to offer. Virginia O'Leary's (1974, p. 815) warning is pertinent: "the adoption of male-valued traits (i.e., rational, analytic orientation) may preclude the development and expression of traits highly valued in the female." Although the institutional supports in making changes are laudable, future efforts should consider women as valuable resources, not potential liabilities. Standards which have been established with a male population need to be revised to include the resources brought by women (Yoder, 1983).

Dominant Group. Changes in the dominant group, male cadets and officers, occurred over time, aiding in the integration of women into the Academy. People assigned to West Point since 1976 expected women to be part of the Corps. When women in the pioneering class arrived in 1976, the all-male classes preceding them had been caught up in the debate about the appropriateness and viability of admitting women. As these classes graduated and new classes took their place, men in each subsequent class held more egalitarian attitudes toward women's roles in society in general (as measured by Spence and Helmreich's, 1972, Attitudes toward Women Scale).

Additionally, institutional policy forbids antifemale expressions, which although seemingly superficial, may be a first step toward changing attitudes by altering, or at least creating an awareness of, discriminatory behaviors (Deutsch & Collins, 1951). We generally think that we need to change people's attitudes in order to change their behaviors. However, cognitive dissonance theory offers us the opposite rationale. According to dissonance theory, when a person holds inconsistent cognitions or beliefs (e.g., I smoke and smoking is hazardous to my health), this creates a negative state of discomfort, called dissonance. In order to reduce this dissonance, the person can either change his or her behaviors (e.g., stop smoking) or psychologically reevaluate the situation (e.g., questioning the applicability of cancer research to anything other than Canadian white rats) (Festinger, 1957).

Using this logic, a similar process may have been activated by policymakers at West Point. If cadets and officers were induced by apparently voluntary means to eliminate antifemale expressions, prejudiced personnel would be left with two inconsistent ideas: (a) we treat women as cadets equal to men (a nondiscriminatory behavior), but (b) we believe that they should not be here (a prejudiced attitude). These people will try to reduce the dissonance this inconsistency creates, but institutional policies will thwart their efforts to change behaviorally. With this avenue of dissonance reduction blocked, these people may psychologically change their attitudes to be consistent with their behaviors; that is, they will develop more egalitarian attitudes. Note that this resolution is possible only if these persons cannot externally justify their nondiscriminatory behavior, for example, by feeling ordered to behave this way. When the Superintendent presented all Academy personnel with the choice to be reassigned, he was setting the stage for personnel to feel that their subsequent behaviors indeed were voluntary. Hence, it may be easier and more effective for practitioners to change attitudes by changing people's behaviors.

Tokens Themselves.   Women at West Point have a natural advantage over tokens in many other institutions. Although female cadets comprise a small percentage of the Corps, they are a formidable group in terms of actual numbers. Unlike the lone token executive, women at the Academy share their experiences with other female classmates. This allows natural social comparison (Festinger, 1954) processes to occur (Darley, 1976). Female support groups are available (Laws, 1975), most notably the women's intercollegiate basketball team and the Corbin seminar, an extracurricular group formed to deal with women's issues. In the Class of 1980, female cadets did not exploit these resources to the fullest, and subsequently, many have left West Point feeling less positive about their experiences than their male counterparts did (Priest, Grove, & Adams, 1980). The availability of support groups is not sufficient. Institutional and peer supports need to demonstrate to women that membership in these groups will have no formal or informal negative consequences and the women themselves need to actively seek out and support each other in spite of the constraints imposed by their token status (Yoder, Adams, Grove, & Priest, in press).

Practitioners may find that positive leadership is possible under most circumstances, with most leaders, and with most followers, *if the situation encourages such leadership.* At West Point, the changes have been dramatic. From 1972 to 1975 when the admission of women to the military academies was hotly debated in Congress (Stiehm, 1981), cadets and officials at West Point, including former Superintendent Lieutenant General Knowlton, argued that there was no place for women at the Academy (Vitters & Kinzer, 1977). However in 1976, 119 women joined the Corps, and of these, 62 graduated four years later. Women will continue to be trained as leaders at West Point and our research has shown that the Academy is more effective at doing this than when tokenism peaked in the early years of coeducation.

SUMMARY

In this chapter, we reviewed recent research on the personality and the situational viewpoints. The work described here was part of Project Athena, a longitudinal study of the integration of women cadets into the United States Military Academy at West Point. Because of the richness of this data set, we were able to consider both models of leadership with the same participants and at the same setting. This consistency afforded comparisons usually unavailable to the researcher of leadership processes.

One would suspect that intelligence would influence leadership in the setting of a military academy, since the Academy includes the functions of a four-year college. Furthermore, the tasks used, writing a proposal and making a scale drawing, require competence on the part of both leaders and followers. The intelligence of the leader affected group performance only when men led groups with traditional sex-role attitudes and performed the structured drawing task. The type of task, followers' attitudes, and the leader's sex acted as screen variables, screening out the influence of the leader's intelligence in other groups. Clearly, the relationship between the leader's characteristics and group performance is not as simple as the personality theorists would like to believe.

We found the same to be true for purely situational theories. Here we saw that the role played by the leader influences followers' appraisals of leadership behavior. For example, when women fill a leadership role that is incompatible with feminine sex-role stereotypes, such as the role of squad leader, followers rate these female leaders lower than they do male leaders. In general, the more sex-inappropriate the leadership role is perceived to be, the more negatively will followers rate the leader.

Situations involve more than interpersonal roles. They also include organizational and societal forces. For example, being a member of a proportionally underrepresented subgroup (referred to as tokens) can create several negative consequences for the token, such as performance pressures and role encapsulation. Policymakers need to be aware of the impact of these situations on individuals in order to maximize the effectiveness of all leaders, male and female.

In general, all the studies presented in this chapter come to the same conclusion: Situations and individuals interact and need to be studied together in order to fully understand leadership processes. Furthermore, both leaders and followers contribute to group performance and morale. The systematic combination of all these factors is discussed in the next chapter.

Chapter 4

Contingency and Transactional Viewpoints

In chapter 3, we discussed several approaches to examining leadership by emphasizing personality and situational elements. Personality factors do influence the leadership process. Also, we recognize that situational influences on leadership are complex and changing. However, neither aspect operates in isolation; rather, they tend to be consistent with each other. We know now with some hindsight that leaders are made, not born. Even though an understanding of the situation helps explain and predict some leadership behaviors, the addition of the situation still does not complete the entire picture of leadership.

Somehow the elements of personality, style, and situation come together and form a process called leadership. Thus, a better understanding of the leadership process is reached by combining personal qualities and behaviors with situational elements. You have just reviewed the evidence of the impact of personality and situational variables separately in chapter 3. We will turn our attention to research which illustrates how the various elements interact together to jointly influence leadership.

In this chapter recent research on contingency and transactional viewpoints will be considered, beginning with the contingency theory. Next, recent research on the model will be presented and critiqued. Then, our focus will shift to the transactional approach to report first-hand research conducted by the authors; the findings will be interpreted as they relate to leader–follower transactions. Recall from chapter 2 that we describe leadership as a dynamic process of mutual influence between the leader and the followers. Empirical research documenting how leaders and followers influence each other toward formal goal attainment and individual need satisfaction is subject to close scrutiny. In summary, the chapter will explain how contingency and transactional approaches help most completely to explain and predict the process of leadership in organizations. The implications for researchers and practitioners will be delineated, setting the framework for the conclusions and future trends.

Once again, all of the research described in this section was conducted at a military setting. The work is an extension of the longitudinal work on Project Athena. The major advantage of this particular study is that we were able to identify patterns of relationships within the same cohesive, functioning groups over an extended period of several years! Unique elements described in this setting, such as sex-roles and sex differences, deserve some particular attention and will be highlighted appropriately in the research findings.

FIEDLER'S CONTINGENCY MODEL

Let us build on our understanding of contingency theory by reviewing some current research that has looked at the effectiveness of contingency theory. Before we begin, it is important to underscore that the key to effective leadership from a contingency approach is the degree to which the leader's style and the appropriateness of the situation are matched. Here we are looking at style as defined in chapter 1, that is, as a trait. It is a predisposition toward a behavioral pattern that is either appropriate or inappropriate within a given situation. Hence, effective leadership is contingent upon the degree to which the leader's style and the situational factors match.

As summarized by several recent review articles of leadership research, Fiedler's contingency theory is one of the most prominent contemporary approaches to leadership (see Hollander, 1978; Jacobs, 1971; Stogdill, 1974; Vroom, 1976). The basic thesis of Fiedler's model is that the relative effectiveness of task-oriented (low LPC) or relationship-oriented (high LPC) styles of leadership is contingent upon situational factors. Within the framework of Fiedler's model, leader style is assessed through the leaders' responses to a least preferred coworker (LPC) scale. Group task performance serves as the criterion of leader effectiveness. The situational variables are treated in terms of the degree to which the leader can influence and control the behavior of group members. This is designated as the situational favorableness dimension. Thus, in operational terms for research, the contingency theory focuses on the relationship between the leaders' LPC score and group task performance as it is moderated by situational factors that affect the influence and control of the leader.

While the importance of the contingency theory is undeniable, the empirical status of predictions generated from contingency theory is a matter of considerable controversy. On one hand, Fiedler and his associates claim that validation studies have generally supported predictions; on the other hand, critics feel that methodological and theoretical inadequacies preclude drawing substantive support for the theory from available research. There have been many different validation studies of the contingency theory of leadership, either in support of Fiedler and his associates work or by critics who found shortfalls, either methodologically or theoretically, with Fiedler's assumptions (see Rice, 1979, for a review of these).

There is no need to repeat that review here. However, it is useful to review briefly arguments for and against the case for generalizability of leadership theory based on research samples of male leaders to those of female leaders. The essence of this argument is the assertion that psychological similarities between men and women outweigh any differences between the sexes. As documented in reviews such as Deaux (1972, 1976a, 1976b) and Maccoby and Jacklin (1974), much research on sex differences has failed to find statistically reliable differences between males and females in terms of most abilities, personality, or performance. Further, in those cases where differences between the scores for men and women do exist, the overlap between the distribution of scores is generally great. Based on the strength of similarities between the sexes, one might anticipate little difficulty in applying the results of male-based research to female leaders. On the other hand, leadership is a process involving more than the characteristics of leaders and followers. It also involves the expectations regarding sex-roles and group norms about sex-appropriate behavior. Hence, it is important for us to suspect that the dynamics of leadership as an influence process with female leaders is sufficiently different than with male leaders, so that findings from research on male leaders are not likely to apply directly to female leaders, and vice versa. We made some discoveries supporting this position in our discussion in chapter 2.

The key to this argument lies in the relational nature of leadership. As Hollander (1978) has argued so persuasively, leadership is not a static personal property; rather, leadership is an interpersonal process between the leader and the followers, a view we also share. From this view one must consider the followers as well as the leader. Especially important are followers' expectations regarding the behavior of the leader. In the case of female leaders, such expectations are likely to be influenced strongly by stereotypes in our cultural setting concerning the behavioral aptitudes and predispositions of women. Finally, the study and understanding of leadership theory using both female and male leaders have theoretical and applied importance beyond simplistic decisions that a theory does or does not generalize to female leaders. Such research can provide an important opportunity to learn more about basic leadership phenomena and the application of leadership theory to the task of organizational effectiveness and development. Thus, we conclude that studies that include both female and male leaders may introduce refinements and extensions to the existing contingency theory. Further, new styles and even theories of leadership may evolve to accommodate the specific concerns of women in leadership roles (as they have done in other areas; see Gilligan, 1982).

PROJECT ATHENA: CONTINGENCY INVESTIGATIONS

As a starting point, Rice, Bender, and Vitters (1980) chose to test Fiedler's contingency model of leadership for its applicability to both female and male leaders. Several reasons for choosing this particular theory should be underscored. The contingency theory has a good amount of notoriety, both in the literature and in practice. There are well-established procedures for testing the theory, including the research questionnaires in chapter 1. There is an explicit link between theory and a program of organizational interventions based on theory. This is another desirable element for using contingency theory in this research. Finally, the controversy surrounding the contingency theory for the last decade gives significance to a validity test for both male and female leaders.

Test of the Contingency Model's Applicability to Men and Women

The design of this study has been described more fully in a technical report by Rice, Bender, and Vitters (1980).[1] The primary aim of the research was to assess the impact of the sex of the leader on two important measures of leadership effectiveness: group task performance and followers' morale. The likelihood of expecting to uncover a relationship between leader gender and the two outcome measures of leadership was appropriate in this study because: (a) the study took place in a masculine-oriented setting involving military leadership training at West Point; (b) sufficient groups of leaders and followers were involved to ensure a stable sample from which to interpret statistical results with confidence; (c) the group tasks required an intense interchange among members in order to obtain an appropriate solution; and (d) separate objective measures of group performance served as an appropriate reference standard for interpreting subjective responses such as followers' morale and perceptions of success.

In the study one half of the groups had male leaders and one half, female leaders. All groups were composed of three male followers. Half of the groups had three followers with traditional attitudes toward women. The remaining groups had three followers with liberal attitudes toward the rights and roles of women in society. The scale used in this study is the same which was described earlier in chapter 2 (see AWS). All groups worked on both a structured and an unstructured task. Performance on the structured task was assessed based on the number of lines correctly placed on an engineer

---

[1]This study involved a laboratory study of 72 groups of male and female leaders working on structured and unstructured tasks. Half of the followers had scores which classify them as traditional in their beliefs and opinions about the rights and roles for women in society. The remaining followers' scores classify them as egalitarian or liberal about women's roles in society.

drawing produced by the group. The unstructured task required that the group prepare a written narrative proposal on how to improve reenlistment percentages in army units.

Before reviewing the major findings from the study, we would also point out that there were two measurements of groups performance: (a) objective scoring of tasks by trained judges using standardized criteria, and (b) a subjective score based upon follow-up surveys. Team morale was measured using Fiedler's (1967) Group Atmosphere Questionnaire. A copy of that scale was described earlier in chapter 1.

The results of the study show several interesting patterns. First, there was a significant relationship between followers' attitudes toward women and the degree of structure involved in the task. The results are shown in Figure 3. The graph clearly shows that groups with followers with traditional attitudes toward women perform better on the structured (drawing) task. Groups composed of followers with more liberal attitudes toward women performed better on the unstructured (proposal) task. Rice et al., (1980) conclude that the statistical significance, shown by the crossing pattern of the lines on the graph, may reflect perceived differences of sex-typing of the tasks. The structured drawing task may fit the stereotype of a masculine task (i.e., spatial arrangements, rapid standard requirements, mathematical calculations, etc.). The unstructured task may appear less masculine in character, because it is a proposal stressing verbal fluency, integration of group ideas, synthesis, and agreement-oriented which may be viewed as consistent with a feminine stereotype.

The results of the group morale index also were quite illuminating. The findings indicate a strong tendency for both leaders and followers to describe group atmosphere more favorably and to report a greater desire to work with

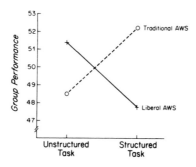

Figure 3.   Mean group performance score as a function of the Follower Attitudes × Task Structure Interaction. From "Leader Sex, Follower Attitudes Toward Women, and Leadership Effectiveness: A Laboratory Experiment" by R. Rice et al., 1980, *Organizational Behavior and Human Performance, 25*, pp. 46–78. Copyright 1980 by The Academic Press. Adapted by permission.

the same group members more after the structured, drawing task than after the unstructured, proposal task. In addition, followers with traditional attitudes toward women described group atmosphere more favorably in groups with male leaders than in groups with female leaders. Finally, followers with more liberal attitudes toward women described group atmosphere similarly in groups with male and female leaders (Rice et al., 1980). These patterns are consistent with the concepts that the AWS scale measures.

Let us examine the implications of these results to the process of leadership. Recall from chapter 1 that task structure and position power of the leader are organizational factors. The drawing assignment was clearly a structured task because its goals are known, and there is only one best objective solution. The proposed task clearly was unstructured.

Position power refers to the degree of legitimate influence the leader possessed. Thus, the more legitimate the authority, the more favorable is that position of leadership. Even if we can assume good leader–member relations, a condition not controlled for in this study, we cannot apply Fiedler's contingency model universally to both men and women since both are facing similar situations. In other words, the study presents compelling evidence that the dynamics of leadership as a process with female leaders is sufficiently different with male leaders and that models like Fiedler's contingency do not adequately take into account the leader sex and sex-role elements.

Test of Sex-Role Congruency with the Contingency Model

In another article based upon additional data collected in the laboratory study involving the same male and female respondents at West Point, Rice, Bender, and Vitters (1982) sought specifically to investigate how valid tests of the contingency model were for men and women. The procedures are identical to those reported in the earlier portion of this chapter.

In this test of the contingency model, attitudes toward women were used as a means of manipulating leader–member relations for women. Rice et al. (1982) developed two hypotheses. The first was: Leader–member relations would be more strained for women leading male followers with traditional sex-role attitudes than for women leading male followers with more liberal attitudes. Because all groups worked on both a structured and unstructured task, Rice and his colleagues assumed that groups with female leaders would be exposed to a wide spectrum of situational favorableness. The second hypothesis to test the contingency model for men and women by Rice et al., (1982) was: The contingency model would be able to accurately predict the relationship between leader LPC score and group performance for both women and men.

In other words, given the assumption that all leaders had low position power, one could provide conditions corresponding to Octants 2, 4, 6, and 8

Table 8
The Contingency Model[a]

	Octant							
	1	2	3	4	5	6	7	8
	Favorable for leader				Unfavorable for leader			
Leader–member relations	Good	Good	Good	Good	Poor	Poor	Poor	Poor
Task structure	Structured		Unstructured		Structured		Unstructured	
Leader position power	Strong	Weak	Strong	Weak	Strong	Weak	Strong	Weak

From *Leadership and Effective Management* (p. 84) by F. E. Fiedler and M. M. Chemers, 1974, Glenview, IL: Scott, Foresman. Copyright 1974 by Scott, Foresman. Reprinted by permission.
[a]The contingency model here shows the situational favorableness for the leader taking in account leader–member relations, whether the nature of the task is structured or unstructured, and in this case focusing on Octants 2, 4, 6, and 8, assuming position power for both male and female leaders is weak.

of the model by crossing good or poor leader–member relations with structured or unstructured tasks. Rice et al., (1982) assumed that all leaders (men and women) had low position power. When you cross this "weak" position power with good or poor leader–member relations and structured and unstructured tasks, we actually create conditions which correspond to Octants 2, 4, 6, and 8 of the model. A diagram of the complete model is presented in Table 8.

The results of the first hypothesis revealed that correlations for male leaders showed a pattern precisely opposite to that for women. That is, the correlations between male leaders' LPC scores and group performance were negative for both structured and unstructured tasks in groups with liberal followers and positive for both structured and unstructured tasks in groups with conservative or traditional followers. The correlations were just the opposite for female leaders. The results of this test do not support the hypothesis. That is, Rice et al., did not find low-LPC female leaders to be relatively more effective in the "most" and "least" favorable conditions. Clearly, these data suggest that the contingency model cannot be applied to female leaders without major changes.

The results of the second test of sex-role agreement with the contingency model also show disappointing results. That is, the relationship between leader LPC score and group performance across the conditions of good and poor leader–member relations was not accurate. What Rice et al. expected to find was strong support for the octant-by-octant predictions in the contingency model. What they found was that for male leaders, two of the four octants were in the direction predicted. For women, three of the four correlations were in the predicted direction. A totai of only five of the eight octant predictions were in the direction expected.

If the researchers assume that the situation was generally more favorable for male leaders than for female leaders, then the results for male leaders can be reinterpreted as with "very favorable" or "moderately favorable." Recall this laboratory study was conducted during the first year women came to West Point. Many male cadets had strong negative attitudes toward the admission of female cadets. In light of this knowledge, a reinterpretation of the favorableness range for men would shorten or eliminate the "unfavorable" situational classification. Finally, Rice and his colleagues admit that the assignment of conditions to Octants 2, 4, 6, and 8 may not be warranted in the second hypothesis. For example, among female-led groups, those with low-LPC leaders were relatively more successful then high-LPC-led groups in Octants 2, 4, and 8. However, none of the three actual correlations just mentioned between leader LPC and group performance were statistically significant. Indeed, the actual situations may have been more favorable than Octants 2, 4, 6, and 8 for male leaders and less favorable for women—thereby bringing in to doubt the meaning of octant-by-octant tests as originally conceived by Fiedler using all male participants.

The discussion and interpretation of these results is difficult and somewhat abstract. We describe these findings with the understanding of the three-dimensional aspect of situational favorableness shown in Table 8. In addition to the three situational variables, leader–member relations, task structure and position power, must be added high- or low-LPC scores for men and women separately. Therefore, Appendix A contains a complete discussion of leader favorableness for each of the eight octant situations. By referring to that detailed description, the results of studies on the contingency model become more straightforward.

Conclusion.   The findings of this contemporary research using military subjects at West Point show two results: (a) one test of the contingency theory suggests that leaders' (LPC) score is often significantly related to the task productivity of the group, and (b) the contingency theory has some weakness with regard to its ability to predict in advance the conditions under which high- and low-LPC leaders are most effective. These two general conclusions regarding the contingency model appear to apply equally well to both male and female leaders.

With regard to the first of the two major findings described earlier, the frequency of significant LPC effects in this study is far beyond what might be expected by chance. Previous research is consistent with this significant conclusion. Concerning the second conclusion, there were serious problems trying to predict in advance the pattern of reliable LPC group performance effects. The match between obtained and predicted associations for each octant of performance (see Table 4 in chapter 1) was not impressive. Only after introducing a post hoc interpretation, proposing different levels of situational favorableness for male and female leaders, is there any general accuracy of the contingency model's ability to predict.

This need for post hoc matching of predicted and obtained results points out, perhaps, the single most important shortcoming of the contingency model relating to male and female leaders. One is never sure of the conditions of any particular study along the dimensions of situational favorableness. Too often the direction and strength of the LPC group performance seem to be a major cue used to assess the degree of favorableness. According to Fiedler's theory, situational favorableness refers to the amount of control and influence the leader has over the group by virtue of the situation. As used by Fiedler, the concept of situational favorableness is far broader and encompasses any variable that affects the leaders' degree of influence and control over the group. Certainly, then, the vertical dyadic linkage of female leaders with either all male or male and female followers continues to exert an impact on the situational favorableness of that leader's influence.

Applicability of Contingency Theory to Female Leaders

Turning now to the general issue of applying contingency theory to women, the results of the present study suggest that considerable caution is necessary. The principal relationship of the contingency model is the association between the leader's LPC and group performance. The studies at West Point frequently showed different patterns for male and female leaders. In many cases, correlations and corresponding conditions had opposite signs for male and female leaders. In conclusion, empirical tests of the type reported here can be more than just sterile reports of old ideas on a new subject population that simply is adding women as leaders. Instead, they can serve as important inputs to better understand the basic phenomenon under study. To some extent, this goal was achieved by the research reported here.

In interpreting the results, the primary focus was on assessing possible differences in terms of impact of situational factors on male and female leaders. In trying to conceptualize such effects, a potential confounding in traditional contingency theory procedures and the importance of developing direct measures of situational favorableness become increasingly apparent.

So where does this leave us? One gap in our understanding of the leadership process is that the contingency theory does not provide for followers' expectations—especially regarding sex-role expectations and stereotypes. We must gravitate more toward a social exchange approach to leadership in considering more complete understanding and appreciation of what actually takes place in the phenomenon called leadership.

Recall from chapter 2 that attending to individual expectations and needs is a function expected from the leader. Leaders' sex type in masculine-sex type positions can disturb the expectations and perceptions that are important in leader–follower transactions. Let us now turn to the transactional approach to demonstrate how clearly this process operates.

PROJECT ATHENA: TRANSACTIONAL VIEWPOINTS

By now you should recognize that leadership is a changing process involving the complexity of several factors. Our focus shifts to the leader, the followers, and the activities that they direct toward the attainment of mutually established goals. This is leader–follower transaction.

Although many leadership studies have relied upon followers' descriptions of leader's behavior, an implicit assumption has been to treat followers as a relatively homogeneous group whose responses can be summed and averaged to determine descriptive actions of the leader (Fleishman, 1973; Fleishman and Simmons, 1970; Halpin, 1954, 1957a, 1957b). The contingency theory approach to leadership has widened the range of factors considered as salient to leadership situations (Fiedler, 1971). The vertical dyadic linkage model rejects the average behavior score in favor of a model which attempts to recognize that leaders react to individual members, not simply to the average group (Graen, Dansereau, Minami, Cashman, 1973). Most recently, studies have given explicit recognition to the possible differential reactions of followers to the leader under similar conditions (Butterfield & Bartol, 1977; Filley, House, & Kerr, 1976; Hartman, 1977). Unfortunately, the results of these studies ask subordinates to describe global behaviors of leader actions—basically, leadership style, or initiating structure and consideration. Whereas it may be argued that followers may describe what they perceive to be leader's behaviors, the investigator may not necessarily understand how effective the leaders are. Thus, the amount of research on followers' reactions to leadership situations suggests that further investigations of "critical incidents" which initiate thoughts of subordinate reactions to leadership situations are needed (Korman, 1973).

Critical Incidents of Good and Bad Leadership

The critical incident technique has been used to study a wide range of phenomena in social and behavioral sciences (Fivars, 1973; Flanagan, 1954). A recent study by Hollander and Neider (1977) and a follow-up by Neider, Carpenter, and Hollander (1979) used this technique to identify dimensions underlying followers' perceptions of good and bad leadership. These studies have used a variety of settings, ranging from undergraduates to supervisors in manufacturing, retail, and community agencies. The results of these studies suggest that categories used to characterize good and bad leadership are specific to organizational settings, i.e., what typifies good leadership in one setting may not necessarily reflect good leadership in a different setting.

As part of the comprehensive leadership research program, Project Athena, conducted at the U.S. Military Academy, followers were asked to write a narrative which describes an example of either good or bad leadership which they observed in summer training. The critical incident technique used in this study asks the followers to describe a specific behavioral episode that represents the presence or absence of the phenomena, good and bad leadership. This free-response format has several advantages over more structured ratings typically used in accessing leader behavior. First, the respondent identifies the qualities and behaviors of the leader that are personally most important, rather than responding to the researcher's preconceived categories. Second, in contrast to the more traditional trait approaches described in the previous chapter, the critical incident technique explicitly examines the behavior of the leader. Moreover, this technique provides information regarding the leader–follower relationship. Finally, a content analysis procedure employed with critical incident research enables the researcher to abstract important underlying dimensions of leader behavior which the followers themselves may not have been able to articulate or conceptualize.

In a study by Adams, Rice, Instone, and Prince (1981, p. 4), followers were asked to provide examples of good leadership using the following instructions:

> Write a narrative description on the back of this questionnaire of an incident that occurred during your summer training experience in which good leadership was displayed. Try to be clear as possible in describing the conditions and behaviors involved. Your narrative should include the positions, but not the names of the people involved, the events leading up to the incident, a description of the incident, why it was good leadership, and how things turned out.

Half the subjects randomly received these instructions. The other half were asked to provide indentical information except that the word "bad" was substituted for "good" in the instructions to the respondent.

The detailed design and tabular information, including reliability coefficients and rater procedures, are provided in a different volume (see Adams, Rice, Instone, & Prince, 1981). The data obtained in this study were analyzed to examine three things: the general characteristics of incidents describing good and bad leadership; a comparison of good and bad leadership descriptions; and a comparison of critical incident descriptions across organizational settings. A complete listing of the leadership categories and the working definitions of the categories is provided in Appendix B.

The results of the general characteristics of incidents reveal several situa-

Table 9
Rank Order of Good Leader Behavior Categories[a]

1. Involvement: Leader actions did or did not reflect personal concern and interest in subordinates' well-being.
2. Motivate: Leader did or did not motivate, encourage, or inspire subordinates to put forth a high level of effort.
3. Downward Communication: Leader did or did not inform subordinates of the rules, duties, goals, and rationale behind various policies.
4. Contingent Sanction: Leader rewards/punishes subordinates as a result of subordinate actions.
5. Role Model: Leader did or did not influence subordinates by example.
6. Unity (cohesiveness): Leader did or did not instill cohesiveness or unity.
7. Upward Communication: Leader did or did not allow subordinates to ask questions, discuss, or relate information to him/her.
8. Expertise: Leader did or did not possess special knowledge or skill.
9. Responsibility: Leader did or did not take responsibility for his/her actions.
10. Noncontingent Sanction: Leader administers rewards/punishments to subordinates without provocation in terms of subordinate actions.
11. Fairness: Leader did or did not treat subordinates similarly.
12. Organize: Leader did or did not organize, structure, or coordinate activities.

[a]A complete coding of these good behavior categories is found in a technical report; see Adams, Rice, & Instone (1981).

tional characteristics describing good leadership. In this case, the follower's sex was sometimes specified. The leader was usually identified as male, a member of the follower's own supervisory organization, and a formal leader. Followers generally described an incident in which they were personally involved and in which the target of the leader's action was the entire group. In addition, descriptions of good leadership seldom mentioned excessiveness,[2] or harassment, or high levels of stress. A rank ordering of good leader behavior categories is provided in Table 9.

The findings for the good leader behavior category revealed that the five most frequently coded categories of good leader behavior included: involvement, motivation, downward communication, contingent sanctions, and role models. In fact 85% of all the leader behaviors in the good leadership condition included these elements. Consequently, it is the presence of these behaviors and the perceived high frequency of these behaviors that characterize good leadership.

However, just as it is important to identify behaviors and qualities associated with good leadership, those behaviors and qualities that followers per-

[2]The term *excessiveness* is a polite way to describe hazing or harassment of a plebe by an upper-class cadet. The Academy has specific policies and regulations which prohibit hazing or harassment. This does not mean that infrequent incidents do not occur. Rather, it only means that institutional policy planners will not tolerate such practices because they serve as dysfunctional consequences of bad leadership.

ceive as not particularly important for good leadership also deserve attention. For example, the leaders' ability to organize, structure, and coordinate activities and treat subordinates fairly (i.e., not show favoritism and reward or punish followers in a manner that is not contingent on their own actions) were described as not characterizing good leadership. While these specific behaviors may indeed represent dimensions of leadership, followers perceptions of these qualities and behaviors indicate that they are not the most important descriptive categories for good leadership in the military setting from which they were taken.

The frequency in which the leader's behaviors were coded in the bad-leadership condition indicates that the bad leader was described as being just as likely to be from the respondents' own organizational element as from someone else's, and was often an appointed leader. For the most part the follower's sex could not be determined. (There was a tendency to relate personally involving incidents, and there were a substantial number of incidents describing episodes involving other persons.) Almost a third of the incidents described a situation in which the leaders' actions were directed at the entire group, while another third were directed at a specific individual.

The incidents of bad leadership almost always made mention of excessiveness or harassment. What followers describe typically as bad leadership and a rank order of the categories most characteristic of bad leadership descriptions is found in Table 10. The top five categories most characteristic of bad leadership include contingent sanctions, noncontingent sanctions, role

Table 10
Rank Order of Bad Leader Behavior Categories[a]

1. Contingent Sanction: Leader rewards/punishes subordinates as a result of subordinate actions.
2. Noncontingent Sanction: Leader administers rewards/punishments to subordinates without provocation in terms of subordinate actions.
3. Role Model: Leader did or did not influence subordinates by example.
4. Downward Communication: Leader did or did not inform subordinates of the rules, duties, goals, and rationale behind various policies.
5. Involvement: Leader actions did or did not reflect personal concern and interest in subordinates' well-being.
6. Fairness: Leader did or did not treat subordinates similarly.
7. Responsibility: Leader did or did not take responsibility for his/her actions.
8. Motivate: Leader did or did not motivate, encourage, or inspire subordinates to put forth a high level of effort.
9. Organize: Leader did or did not organize, structure, or coordinate activities.
10. Upward Communication: Leader did or did not allow subordinates to ask questions, discuss, or relate information to him/her.
11. Expertise: Leader did or did not possess special skill or knowledge.
12. Unity (cohesion): Leader did or did not instill cohesiveness or unity.

[a]The bad-leader categories were adopted from the same sources as the good-leader categories.

model, downward communication, and involvement. Basically, these five categories represent 86% of the behaviors of bad leadership. Again, it is the absence or excessive use of these behaviors that followers perceive as important in these descriptions of bad leadership.

There are several ways to summarize the findings. First, consider the general tendency for good leadership incidents to be characterized by situations in which the follower was personally involved with the leader from his or her own organization. Several plausible explanations can be offered for this pattern. These results closely parallel the positive attributional bias found in previous investigations of leadership at West Point. Adams, Rice, Instone, and Prince (1980) reported an attributional bias in which cadets reported successful group performance to the leader but perceived unsuccessful performance as not being caused by the leader. These results formed a positive correlation between perceived success of the unit and the strength of belief that the leader was a major contributor to unit performance. These prior data, in conjunction with the present results, suggest that people have a positive bias toward leadership. Contrary to some common-sense notions, these followers do not generally complain about bad leadership in their own units or blame the leader for poor unit performance. Instead, they see bad leadership as more prevalent in other units and credit good performance of their own unit to the leader. Not only is this pattern of behavior found within a particular military setting, but there is also a strong desire among followers or cadets to compete and try to beat other units. This interpretation will support earlier research findings on intra- and intergroup competition that Blake and Mouton (1962b) and Blake, Mouton, and Sloma (1964) reported in their studies in nonmilitary settings.

Another interpretation focuses on the typical role relationships of the followers in this structured organization. In terms of leader–follower interactions, the target of the leader's action revealed a great deal about leader style. In general, followers described an individual leader interacting with the entire group in the good leadership condition but with individual followers in the bad leadership condition. These results suggest that good leadership is more often characterized by an average leadership style of leader–follower interations and bad leadership by a vertical dyadic leadership relationship or between the leader and a specific follower. The average leadership style is one in which it is assumed that the leader behaves in a similar manner to all subordinates and in which all subordinates are sufficiently similar to be considered as a single entity. On the other hand, the vertical dyad linkage model holds each subordinate follower–superior relationship to be unique.

By way of possible explanations, the nature of the leader–follower exchange may be one in which positive interactions are shared with the subordinate group, i.e., the leader will praise the entire group together. But individual accomplishments as a norm are played down so as to avoid devisiveness within the group. On the other hand, negative interactions (i.e., a leader reprimanding subordinates) may be of a more personal and private nature and, thus, these incidents are reported as bad leadership and harassment. Here the leader is seen as focusing attention toward one individual rather than upon the group.

The applications of this research support and extend research conducted by Hollander and his associates. Two general areas derived from a comparison of these studies merit special attention: (a) situational specificity of follower perceptions of good and bad leadership, and (b) the relationship between the critical incident technique and the more traditional rating scales.

One of the ongoing controversies in leadership research is whether there are global characteristics associated with good and bad leadership or whether these characteristics are specific to the population under investigation (Stogdill, 1974). In other words, are the qualities that define a good or bad leader in one situation the same qualities that define a good or bad leader in a different situation? In order to answer this question, the results from content analyses of critical incident descriptions can be compared with those obtained from different organizational settings.

Interestingly, five categories of leader behavior qualities emerge as important in both military and civilian settings: organization, motivation, expertise, cohesiveness, and fairness. Similarity between the classification systems in the military and civilian research argues for the existence of some behaviors which generalize across several situations. On the other hand, the differences between these classification systems support the usefulness of the critical incident technique for setting specific typologies. In civilian organizations involving nonmilitary research, it was often the presence of a few specific leader behaviors that best typified good leadership and the lack or misuse of these same behaviors that exemplified bad leadership. Also, this was true in the study at West Point. Four of the five top categories were common to descriptions of both good and bad leadership. These results suggest that it is the presence or absence of a few situationally specific leader behaviors that best connote good and bad leadership.

Future Research with Critical Incidents.   Since the critical incident technique is especially useful to determine leadership typologies to be tailored to the unique elements of each organization, an area for future research concerns the applicability and generalizability of the results obtained in this study to other military and civilian settings. A second area meriting additional research concerns the potential gender differences in descriptions of good and bad leadership. The sex typing variable was difficult to measure in the present study because of an inability both to identify the gender of the persons involved in the majority of the incidents and to have respondents select female leaders. There is already some evidence that leaders' behaviors and characteristics identified by the critical incident techniques differ with the sex of the persons involved (see Hollander & Neider, 1978). A subsequent follow-up however, failed to replicate these results (Neider, Carpenter, & Hollander, 1979). Since the issue of gender differences is an important one to understand the process of leadership, a more comprehensive analysis which includes gender as a factor would help to clarify whether the behaviors characterizing good and bad leadership differ with the sex of those involved in the incident.

Gender, Social Power, and Leader–Follower Relationships

There are several studies of the relationship between the outcome measures of leadership success and the process variables of social power and influence (e.g., Ayers-Nachamkin, Cann, Reed, & Horne, 1982; Lord, 1977). However, there is very little research examining the effect of leader gender on this relationship. Presently, we will discuss a study designed to explore this relationship by correlating subordinates' reports of leaders' success with the process variables of social power and influence from men and women, separately. In addition, two sets of factors were used to represent processes of social power and influence: (a) the reasons cited for complying with the directives, and (b) suggestions of the leader and the perceived frequency with which the leaders used specific strategies in their attempts to influence subordinates. Basically, we tried to determine the social power and influence processes through which males and females attain success. Earlier we noted that the relationship between leader with followers, which we call the transactional process, also takes into account the situation, that is, the social structure, roles, task demands, and patterns of emergence of leaders.

This particular study, again borrowing from an empirical base derived and tested at West Point under Project Athena, gives us some insight on how social power and influence relates to leadership success for male and female leaders. How a leader emerges will influence the dynamics of the leadership process. As will be evident shortly, the leadership process differs when the leader's sex is added to this transactional relationship.

Based upon previous theory and research, it is possible to develop hypotheses corresponding with several questions motivating the conduct of the study reported here. However, two general themes from the previous literature played particularly important roles in developing propositions. These are sex-role stereotypes and sex differences in social status.

In chapter 2 we described the influence of stereotypes particularly in the sense that males are generally described by adjectives such as independent, objective, assertive, unemotional, and active, whereas females are generally perceived as dependent, subjective, nurturant, passive, and emotional. It is also clear that males often hold positions of authority in Western society and that they are ascribed a higher social status than females (Johnson, 1978). Let us suppose that stereotypes and status differences can be translated into leader sex differences when subordinates or followers describe their leaders. If this is so, we could offer the following propositions:

1. Males are perceived by their followers as being more successful leaders than females in male-dominated tasks.
2. Followers' descriptions of the leadership process associated with male and female leaders are consistent with sex-role stereotypes, sex differences, and status. Also, female leaders will be attentive to upward communications from their subordinates. Males will be more effective in communicating directives, objectives, rules, and related information downward to their followers.
3. Females leaders will more frequently employ indirect, nonconfrontational influence tactics such as helplessness, personal reward, hinting, and the like. Male leaders will more often use direct influence tactics that perhaps rely on claimed expertise, authority, or stated rationale.

We may even extend this statement to the fact that followers of female leaders will be more likely to comply on a basis of formal positional powers, that is, legitimate, coercive, or reward powers. Followers of male leaders will be more likely to comply on a basis of personally maintained powers, such as reference expert and information.

We already know from chapter 2 that attribution outcomes involve factors both internal and external to the leader as causes for performance in male- versus female-led groups. Will the followers ascribe more luck to women in successful outcomes and recognize the personal success of male contributions? The details of the design and methodology used for the conduct and analysis of this study can be found in Rice, Instone, and Adams (1984). Many things can be discussed in a study this complex, but within the realm of transactional approaches to leadership we will highlight those that bear most on the hypotheses and our understanding of this leadership process.

It is important to keep in mind that leadership is a social exchange process involving the leader and his or her followers. It is not a personal property of the leader. In examining the nature of this transactional process, the most overwhelming finding is that the leader's sex was not a significant factor in the study. This study found that whether the leader was male or female had no influence on 90% of the tests conducted. Of the few significant results where leader sex emerged, its magnitude was not great in that less than 2% of the variance was explained. In essence then, if we look at Proposition 1, the followers are saying that males are not perceived as being more successful than are females. With regard to Propositions 2 and 3, the subordinates' descriptions of the process associated with the male and female leaders were not consistent with sex-role stereotypes, sex differences, and status. Typically, they did not expect female leaders to be more accessible to upward communication or male leaders to be more influential in downward directive communications. Finally, women were not reported as using more indirect, nonconfrontational influence tactics. Males did not show any statistically larger degree of direct influence relying on expertise, authority, or personal basis of power. Factors associated with internal or external attributions of luck for females' successes did not appear in any meaningful pattern here. Thus, none of the three general hypothesis based on sex-role stereotypes and social status differences were supported by these data.

Obviously, the lack of statistical significance here has immense practical utility. These results indicate that the leader's sex was not a variable of importance in this particular study. In fact, it is noteworthy that strong and replicable leader-sex effects failed to emerge, given the methods employed in this research (Cohen & Burns, 1978). For example, two particular summer training sessions were used, and in neither case did gender differences or leader-sex effects emerge. However, recent research from a variety of other settings suggests that failure to detect strong leader-sex effects is not particular to military settings. Szilagyi (1979) failed to find substantial differences in the extent to which male and female supervisors made their actions contingent upon subordinates' behavior. Similarly, Hall and Donnell (1979) failed to find substantial leader-sex effects in their broad spectrum of assessment of over 900 female and male managers of comparable background and status. Butterfield and Powell (1981, p. 130) summarized such conclusions succinctly: "It is now commonly believed that actual (leader sex) differences in the behavior of real leaders are virtually nonexistent." The results of the present research are best viewed as adding support to the growing body of evidence supporting this particular conclusion.

Implications for Researchers and Practitioners

Before summarizing the findings of both contingency and transactional theories, the implications of the research reviewed for future researchers and practitioners must be considered.

For Researchers.   Several ideas for future research can be gleaned from the preceding discussion. First, much of the understanding of leadership has been conducted by male investigators using male subjects. Models have been posited and predictions based on how males would interact with other males in an organizational setting. In the changing society of the 1980s and 1990s, however, sex typing of the groups will be mixed increasingly. It will not be uncommon to see many more female leaders as well as a more balanced mix of male-female followers. The degree to which gender and sex-role stereotyping influence these models is a matter of great concern in leadership research (Garland & Price, 1977; Touhey, 1974). Some of the early results involve laboratory studies of sex-role stereotypes and sex differences in leadership. Osborn and Vicars (1976, p. 447) summarize the saliency of the early findings:

> Artificial short-term laboratory situations tend to elicit subject responses based on readily available stereotypes, while long-term, real life, field settings include extensive interpersonal contact that provide subjects with a more realistic basis for their behavior. Thus, lab studies may yield deceptive data in overstating the total influence of sex stereotyping.

The present studies reported in this volume have consistently failed to demonstrate biases in sex-role stereotyping and in sex differences among leaders. We fully subscribe to the belief that the interaction patterns involving the subjects in this research were consistently more long-term and realistic, thereby, providing the leader–follower dynamic with valid information, allowing them to move beyond sex-role stereotypes in their responses. Such factors, we believe, influence both the judgments of leaders' success and attribution of group performance. In future research it will be valuable to bear in mind the insightful conclusion of Osborne and Vicars (1976).

For Practitioners.   The general absence of strongly biased results in these data reported in contemporary studies of contingency and transactional leadership reflects both institutional encouragement of gender fairness and the preparation of female leaders. Organizations which have been sensitized to the issue of gender bias and which may be involved in taking affirmative action to handle such problems are probably in the forefront of full integration of women in leadership roles. In looking at the success reported in the military, West Point can refer to a comprehensive program (Project Athena), numerous reports, workshops, and interventions around sex-role stereotyping which have helped to reeducate both leaders and followers regarding the feasibility of men and women working collaboratively toward institutional goals. Investment in such programs can be considerable, depending on the number of female leaders. However, the long-term rewards for such an investment cannot be ignored.

We have seen that leaders do not merely achieve legitimacy based upon their appointed status. Designated leaders may not readily enjoy the support of their followers in the way that proven leaders do. The longitudinal nature of the Athena program has allowed an emergent leadership process to take place. Both male and female leaders in multiple trials by fire are required to demonstrate their leadership performance to their peers, superiors, and followers. This convergent comparison allows for the most favorable nurturing condition for leadership. This occurs when leaders demonstrate their confidence in an emergent sense, and then, at the end of their final training program (in this case, four years), are elected or appointed to a legitimate status, either as the ranking cadets to run the Corps of Cadets or as newly appointed officers to join the U.S. Army. This high degree of participation and apparent motivation reflected in emergence, combined with the legitimacy and support, have helped these leaders to become successful.

SUMMARY

In this chapter, we have discussed leadership from two contemporary and popular viewpoints: contingency and transactional. We reviewed briefly some major assumptions of contingency theory in light of recent evidence from studies involving male and female leaders. We noted that there may be serious problems to try to predict a priori reliable LPC group performance influences. Indeed, many measures of strength of association showed different patterns for male and female leaders. Clearly, situational favorableness (amount of control and influence the leader has over the group) demonstrates that leader–follower relationships are more complex when mixed sex typing is involved.

Sex-roles and leader sex can be variables whose influence may wane over time. As noted in chapter 2, sex-roles and sex differences exert an impact on the leadership process. However, this chapter reports that these variables may be "controlled" in organizations which have been committed to reducing sex and gender biases. Initially, designated female leaders may not readily enjoy the compliance of followers the way that male leaders do. However, proven leaders, be they male or female, enjoy the support of followers even to the point of overshadowing stereotypic beliefs and attitudes about women in leadership.

Chapter 5

Conclusion: The Need for Synthesis

In this chapter, we will bring together several loose ends and synthesize our discussion so far. We began this book by examining leadership, first as theorists and then as practitioners. Next, we looked at a series of research projects at the U.S. Military Academy in order to further explicate leadership within a concrete setting, to make suggestions for enhancing positive leadership for policy makers, and to suggest future avenues of study for researchers. Let us take a brief look at what we learned.

Throughout the book, we have talked about an evolving program of understanding leadership as a phenomenon and as a process. The initial focus was on the individual and the "great man" theories which pointed naturally to research on personal characteristics and traits. Consumers of this information eventually saw the need to move beyond traits to specific actions, and later still, to particular actions under specific situations. Finally, we were able to bring about a synthesis of this information which is based upon an interaction of persons and situations built around role attainment, contingencies, and how leaders and followers see each other. Now, we will explore ways to narrow the gap between the academician conducting pure research and the practitioner facing the exigencies of real life.

CONTRIBUTIONS OF PERSONALITY AND SITUATIONAL APPROACHES

One major point of chapter 3, was that personality and situational approaches were not simply the remnants of the history of leadership research. Rather, some current researchers actively developed hypotheses derived from both personality and situational theories and tested these in the laboratory and the field. One such hypothesis was the screen model of Fiedler and Leister (1977). They hypothesized that some factors screen out the relationship between leaders' personality characteristics and their effectiveness. Specific screen variables, such as stress with one's superiors, sex-role stereotyping of the leader's role, followers' expectations, and characteristics of the group's task, were identified by subsequent research.

These findings can be tied together by understanding the situation they create. In considering these research projects, one conclusion is that each significant screen variable affects the favorability of the situation for the leader. The personality characteristics of leaders, such as their intelligence, are positively related to group performance *only when* the situation is favorable. When the task is structured, when the leader fits our societal stereotype of a male leader, when followers' hold traditional attitudes toward sex-roles, or when stresses with the boss are minimal, then, and only then, is the intelligence of the leader positively correlated with group performance.

On the other hand, when the circumstances of leadership are less favorable, the personality traits of leaders play no role in determining their effectiveness. This may be true because leaders' qualities are diluted in the wake of other adversities. When the group is confronted with other concerns, such as the sex-role inappropriateness of a female leader, group members will concentrate on this role violation rather than on the leader herself. This behavior is exhibited because the group members must rely on past values, expectations, and perceptual sets about what is appropriate and who can appropriately perform in given prescribed positions. When these external, circumstantial difficulties are minimized, the leader may stand forward as an object of scrutiny. Under these favorable circumstances, the qualities of the leader, such as intelligence, rise to the forefront and, hence, affect group processes.

This research suggests that the personality qualities of female leaders do little to enhance or diminish their effectiveness. This may leave female leaders, by virtue of their sex, feeling powerless to influence group processes. As the research shows, this indeed may be the only conclusion possible within the structure of our current society and the sex-role stereotypes it generates and maintains. The key may not be in training women themselves to display the supposed characteristics of successful leadership by women. Rather, the focus of change may be placed better on the situation itself. This may entail a reevaluation of what characterizes positive leadership, a significant reduction of sexism in our society, and the encouragement of egalitarian attitudes among both women and men. These are no small chores. However, this research suggests that the simple conformity of women to the principles of effective leadership developed for men will ignore the circumstantial factors that will screen out the effects of personality traits.

In chapter 3, we argued that a situation-centered perspective to social change is advantageous because of the ethical and practical constraints involved in attempting to change individuals. Furthermore, both transactional and contingency research illustrate the importance of situational variables in affecting leadership effectiveness. Policymakers at West Point have directed their energies toward changing institutional policies, dominant group members, and the tokens themselves in order to design situations that encourage positive leadership. With this specific work as our base, let us consider more general ideas about how situation-centered change can be enacted.

The situation in which leadership occurs can be classified along a dimension of scope which at one end extends outward to broad societal influences and which focuses inward on organizational factors and finally, on interpersonal exchanges. As we shall see in chapter 7, leadership takes place within a given society, within a specific organization, and between a particular leader and his or her followers. The characteristics of each of these levels of the situation ultimately filter down to influence the leadership process as it is enacted by given individuals. Examination of each of these levels of the situation may help bring them to life.

Improving Leadership Effectiveness at the Microscopic Level

At the microscopic level, a leader interacts with his or her followers within an immediate context. Different expectations clearly are assumed for leaders who perform different tasks, from basketball coaches to military officers to production-line supervisors. One characteristic of such tasks, their structure, has been explored extensively by contingency theorists. Another central characteristic of leadership at this level is the interpersonal relations developed between a leader and his or her followers. As we have seen, both contingency and transactional theories have stressed the importance of this factor in affecting leadership effectiveness.

The organizational context also is influential (Figure 2, chapter 2). At this level, we need to consider the structure of the organization (such as its degree of formality) and its relationships with other organizations with which it competes or cooperates. Finally, all organizations exist within a societal context which places economic, sociocultural, and legal–political demands on the organization's functioning. Let us consider what researchers and practitioners may want to understand at each of these levels as they envision situational changes geared to improving leadership.

Interpersonal Levels. Two aspects of the situation are important to readers interested in improving leadership at the microscopic level: technical-task and interpersonal concerns. Structured tasks contribute to overall situational favorability. Well-structured tasks are ones in which goals are clear, where there is only one best solution, and where feedback will verify the correctness of a decision. All tasks need not be this clear; however, the task atmosphere will be enhanced to the extent that goals are well-defined and attainable. In addition to task characteristics, interpersonal relations between leaders and followers contribute significantly to the immediate work atmosphere. Humanistic industrial psychologists are interested in changing these role relations in order to bring about improved leadership patterns. For example, Argyris (1976) describes "double-loop learning" which is aimed at changing the values and assumptions of effective leaders. According to Argyris, there are two basic models to which a leader may explicitly or implicitly adhere. There are four governing values associated with Model I: (a) achieve goals as they are defined; (b) win, never lose; (c) hide negative feelings; and (d) stress rationality. The consequences of holding these sets of values are: (a) defensiveness; (b) rigidity; (c) little risk-taking; and (d) ultimately, decreased effectiveness.

In contrast, a leader following Model II values: (a) valid information; (b) free and informed choice; and (c) internal commitment. Consequently, this leader: (a) is minimally defensive; (b) is open to feedback; (c) publicly tests his or her theories; and (d) is willing to share power. This pattern of assumptions directs leaders toward double-loop learning. This model of learning parallels the scientific model in which hypotheses are formulated and tested, feedback is given, and then, based on these results, the hypotheses are evaluated and alternatives are considered.

Argyris (1976) presents research and theory directed toward helping individuals to change their theories of action to reflect Model II values. It is through such changes that humanistic industrial psychologists plan to improve leadership exchanges between the leader and group members. Argyris argues that technical competency among leaders is not sufficient for effective leadership; rather, upgrading both technological and interpersonal skills are important to enhance the situational favorability of the immediate context of effective leadership.

A more focused examination of role relations among leaders and followers concentrates on the expectancies held by both leaders and followers that the leaders' sex brings to the immediate situational context. Transactional theory predicts that such expectations will influence effective leadership. For practitioners interested in creating microscopic situational favorability, an argument can be supported for changing standards to avoid biases against either sex and to bring out the best qualities of both women and men.

As seen throughout this book, expectations about leadership incorporate many masculine and few feminine traits (Massengill & DiMarco, 1979; Schein, 1973). Because of this, the standard against which effective leadership frequently is evaluated is one which has been developed for and by men. In fact, in chapter 3 when the task became more stereotypically masculine (military squad leader), the ratings of the leadership performance of women declined in comparison with those of male cadets. This research suggests that standards of evaluation of effective leadership often are biased against women by virtue of their sex and the gender-trait expectations that accompany it.

The point of this analysis is that standards of effectiveness need to be evaluated and, where necessary, improved to remove discriminatory biases against women. This requires that women not be regarded as liabilities but rather as resources that can be encouraged to extend and better our current criteria for judging good leadership (O'Leary, 1974). Specific suggestions for altering these standards as they affect professional women are offered by Friedan (1981) who calls for flex-time options and less geographic relocations. These alternatives imply that work life is only one aspect of a professional's life and that satisfaction among career-oriented men and women will be heightened by improvements in the overall quality of life (Davis & Cherns, 1975; Hackman & Suttle, 1977).

Since Friedan (1981) discusses professional women, let us use this as a case in point. All professions (e.g., lawyer, physician, and professor) demand at least three years of postgraduate work and/or some sort of additional training beyond the graduate degree, such as an internship. Consider the age at which these demands are made. The twenty-one-year-old, first-year graduate student faces at least four years of graduate school and, if an academic career is pursued, six years until tenure is granted (at best). This means that career demands will be central for this person at least until age thirty-one. For a woman, these years cover the best of her reproductive years. Additionally, the pursuit of such a career by older women as well as men often is discouraged. Are such demands inherently biased against women? And, more importantly, need they be this way?

According to Rossi (1976), acceptance of these standards as unchanging reflects a pluralist model of society that is conservative in orientation. An egalitarian solution to this dilemma is to assimiliate women into the existent social structure. The assimiliation model assumes that female leaders need to be retrained; this is a solution we already have discarded. Finally, with a hybrid model, we seek to change the structure of our society to benefit both men and women. Such a restructuring can begin at this microscopic level of the leadership process by changing the standards of evaluation used to judge effective leadership. For example, by using Friedan's (1981) idea about relocation with some modification, management could disassociate some promotions from geographic relocations, and hence allow both male and female employees to develop their families and careers within a stable community.

In sum, researchers and practitioners interested in making situational improvements at the microscopic level generally focus on two aspects of the immediate situation: technical–task and interpersonal. Contingency theory has provided much information about the influence of task characteristics, in particular, task structure, on leadership effectiveness. Both contingency and transactional theories point to leader–member relations as an important component of the leadership processes. The training program of Argyris

(1976) designed to teach effective leadership by enhancing these interpersonal relations is an example of microscopic work geared to improving the effectiveness of leaders by changing the immediate situational context.

Improving Leadership Effectiveness at the Macroscopic Level

Organizational Structure. A good examination of the structural components of an organization and their influence on effective leadership is presented in Kanter's (1977) book. One aspect of the organization's composition, tokenism, was discussed earlier. Numerically underpresented group members face a negative situation that needs to be improved in order for the token to succeed. One focus for such change is upon institutional policies which can be restructured so that all group members stand to benefit from the successes of the token.

Other important characteristics of the organization uncovered by Kanter (1977) involve opportunity and power. As with tokenism, Kanter argues that what we previously regarded as real sex differences are most often differences between men and women created by differing situations. For example, women often are chastised for not exhibiting the same degree of career commitment as shown by men. This has led some people to conclude that women possess inadequate needs for achievement (Adams, Priest, & Prince, in press; Hedrick & Chance, 1977; Horner, 1972; Stein & Bailey, 1973).

Kanter (1977) submits that it is not one's sex per se that causes this effect, but rather this apparent sex difference is the result of differential situational contingencies faced by women and men. She points out the perceived lack of opportunities for advancement reported by many women in the business she studied and concludes that it is these artificial headwinds confounded within promotion practices that lie at the root of women's lack of career commitment.

Evidence supports the claim that situational factors underlie apparent sex differences in career commitment. Women's perceptions of discrimination in advancement policies and procedures and women's career aspirations are significantly correlated. In other words, women who feel that biases exist that mediate against the promotion of women also report low career commitment. Kanter herself (1977, p. 161) shows that when men face a work setting in which their own chances for advancement appear jeopardized, these men also exhibit low career commitment. Hence, Kanter's conclusion extends to men confronted with the situational conditions concerning promotion opportunities that often face women.

Note the orientation of the above argument. No one is blaming women for alleged inadequacies arising from either their physiology or their socialization (Ryan, 1976; Yoder, 1983). Rather, situational characteristics, in this case those of the organization, are examined, focusing on how they impact upon the behaviors and attitudes of both men and women. Most importantly, change agents can direct their activities toward ethical and realistic improvements by designing positive and unbiased situations. In the example described by Kanter (1977), policies regarding promotion can be scrutinized and modified to enhance the opportunities for all employees within an organization.

Societal Changes. At the broadest level of situational analysis are societal factors. These span factors that go beyond the organization to the context in which the organization operates. Examples of these larger variables are sociocultural factors, economic influence, and legal–political contingencies.

Sociocultural factors include both formal and informal education, with the latter generally referred to as socialization. Socialization is the process through which we learn the norms of our culture. Norms are general expectations about how people should behave in all situations. A basic norm in our society describes the nuclear family as one in which the man is the breadwinner and the woman with children does not work outside the home. As Friedan (1981) points out, although the social norm dictates against working mothers, only a small minority (about 11%) of American families actually conform to this norm. In fact, a history of working women in this century shows that actual behavior and this particular social norm generally have not been compatible (Chafe, 1977).

However, this norm influences how working women are treated. Although there is evidence that many women work because of economic necessity, there continues to be an assumption that women work for extra money and therefore can be paid less than men for the same job. This is recognized in the current, popularized revelation that women earn, on the average, 62 cents for every dollar earned by a man (this figure is for 1983). Furthermore, this figure reflects a recent drop in women's earnings (e.g., in 1955 women earned 64 cents for every dollar collected by men; National Organization for Women, 1981b).

A similar analysis can be made regarding another popular expectation about working women—that they will quit their jobs when familial obligations demand their full attention (Broverman, Vogel, Broverman, Clarkson, & Rosenkrantz, 1972). As the number of working mothers increases (52% of wives currently hold jobs outside the home; National Organization of Women, 1981a), this expectation loses its support. Furthermore, studies of why women leave their jobs offer additional provocative information.

For example, Llewellyn (1981) studies the employees at a bank. One obvious statistic that Llewellyn calculated showed that women did not remain in their jobs as long as their male counterparts. Here are the data so frequently used to justify the expectation that women are not reliable employees. However, this conclusion soon became suspect in light of Llewellyn's findings. She found that because employers held this expectation, they recruited less qualified women, paid them less, discouraged them from taking examinations necessary for promotion, used them to train incoming men, and, in the end, promoted women less frequently and after longer time periods than men. Kanter's admonition about deficient promotion opportunities readily comes to mind. Is the bank closing opportunities for women and hence causing them to leave their jobs? Could employers' expectations cause these behaviors which, in turn, reinforce their expectations? If so, this is quite a vicious cycle. Although there are no definitive answers to these questions at this time, evidence exists to support them as viable hypotheses. Clearly, chances for challenging and fruitful work in this area are available for the asking.

Similar analyses can be proposed for other aspects of the societal context in which organizations function. For example, studies of different patterns of leadership across economic systems would be informative (Bass, 1977; Bennis, 1976; Green, 1977). Do leaders work differently in capitalist as opposed to socialist countries? It is to global questions such as these that sociologists and anthropologists might address their attention.

Conclusion. The personality and situational viewpoints have contributed to the massive body of past and present research on leadership. Specifically, we have seen that personality characteristics do affect group processes when circumstantial factors do not interfere. Furthermore, the situational theories point to three promising areas for future development: (a) the transaction involved in interpersonal roles, (b) organizational structures, and (c) societal influences. These last points should be of particular interest to practitioners, because it is pragmatic and ethical to envision situational changes that will improve leadership.

CONTRIBUTIONS OF CONTINGENCY AND TRANSACTIONAL APPROACHES

In looking at the contributions of contingency theory in chapter 4, there can be no doubt that there is disappointingly little empirical evidence that traits and behavioral categories by themselves predict leadership performance (see Campbell, Dunnette, Lawler, & Weick, 1970). As we have seen already, the effectiveness of leaders will depend upon the situation. As Fiedler (1967) has stated, people behave differently at funerals than they would at cocktail parties. The problem at issue then is whether the tendency to behave in a particular situation is an attribute of the leader's personality and thus properly considered that person's style. Alternatively, one could ask whether the leader's personality and the situation interact and whether the person's behavior under one condition tends to be relatively less predictable in another situation. That is the issue which spawned much of the leadership theory described in chapter 1. Applying the knowledge derived from contingency theory in the 1960s and early 1970s showed great promise to managers. However, societal changes for the rights and roles for women caused a search back into the theoretical realm to see if literature and thought were appropriate to the changing times, and, hence the newly studied influence of sex-role and sex difference variables discussed in chapter 2.

Perhaps the major contribution described in chapter 4 as relates to contingency theory is how generalizable that particular theoretical approach is to both female and male leaders. We recognize that one camp would argue that sex differences have failed to reveal many statistically significant differences in terms of abilities, personality, and performance. And indeed where differences were noted, the overlap of the distribution of the range of scores for women and men as separate groups was great. Clearly, given these similarities between sexes, one might expect to have little difficulty in applying male-based research to female leaders.

On the other hand, leadership is a process that not only involves unique personal characteristics of leaders but also involves expectations about what is appropriate leader behavior. Hence, sex-typing of certain tasks may create different expectations of male than female leaders. The primary aim of the research described in chapter 4 was to assess the impact of sex of the leader on measures of leadership or group effectiveness. The results did not support the position of generalizability of leadership from male to female leaders. What we found was a gap between the old theory and today's practice.

Closing the Gap Between Old Theory and Contemporary Practice

Managers were applying untested principles and findings to a radically different situation than was originally considered in contingency theory development. There were significant relationships between followers' attitudes toward women and how structured the drawing task was. The structured task perhaps fits the stereotype of a masculine sex-typed task involving quantification of scores, special spatial arrangements, and an objectively measured outcome. These actions stereotypically describe a group or work setting that more frequently involved men than women.

Another finding which signaled a gap between old theory and contemporary practice was that group morale results tended to reveal that followers with traditional attitudes toward women's roles described group atmosphere as being more favorable for male leaders than female leaders. Finally, the most explicit test of the contingency model and its ability to predict octant-by-octant relationships between leaders' LPC scores and group performance was tested for men and women. Remember that the findings reported that the pattern of correlations of male leaders' scores with group performance was precisely opposite the pattern found for women! On the face of such evidence, one could not conclude that the contingency model, as it stands, is an effective theory applicable equally to both women and men.

Even a second test of sex-role agreement with the contingency model did not show a matched pattern for men and women. Examining LPC scores with "good leader–member relations" was not confirmatory. That is, there was no strong support for the capability of the contingency model to make accurate octant-by-octant predictions. Recall that the contingency model offers specific predictions between leader LPC and group performance for each of the eight octants or conditions classified in terms of three situational factors. Indeed, the nature of the contingent relationships between leader's LPC and group performance may be different for males and females (e.g., task-oriented females may perform most effectively in situations of moderate or intermediate favorableness, even though the model says that relation-oriented men are thought to perform most effectively in such situations).

These findings taken together cast into doubt the original octant-by-octant test as originally conceived by Fiedler using male participants. Also, the results of these studies show that the model cannot be applied uniformly to female leaders without some changes. Lastly, what these results mean for practitioners is that different behaviors are evoked by the situation as it becomes "less favorable," less controllable, and perhaps more threatening.

As Fiedler (1967) says, if we visualize each person as having a hierarchy of goals which each person seeks to attain, it then seems reasonable to assume that the person will attempt to secure the goal which is most important. A situation might be quite threatening to one person, but it presents little or no threat to another individual. The novelty of introducing women into a male-dominated task (military leadership) where followers have basically traditional attitudes toward women's roles seems to demonstrate exactly this kind of example.

The contingency theorists would recommend to managers that, indeed, not everyone will perform well in the same situation. Thus, the argument is set forth that you must match each person's leader style with the appropriate situation. For some, this could be a similar job. For others, it might mean a new position which would provide the proper challenge. To the manager or the practitioner, such a recommendation would mean a very detailed planning, assignment, and rotation policy in order to improve the performance of many people in the organization. Whereas the idea is one that makes sense, the practical execution of such a complex program in a large organization and the inherent training costs involved would make such a training solution questionable. We must look for a more comprehensive approach to understanding the leadership process.

Hollander (1978) introduced that earlier in chapter 2 when we described the transactional approach. Conceptually, his theory is different from situational and contingency approaches. Recall that there is an interaction which describes a person-to-person relationship in which one person's behavior influences another. The transactional nature refers to a two-way process, and in the presence of social exchange, both leaders and followers expect give and take.

The transactional approach draws as a natural extension of the contingency theory. Initially, the situational approach was a logical step away from the emphasis on leader traits which long dominated the study of leadership. In a way, the situational approach paved the way for the contingency approach, which added followers to the formula to create the transactional viewpoint.

In itself, the situational viewpoint treated leaders and the situation as if they were separate. This caused one gap in our understanding of leadership and its practice, because it overlooked the fact that the leader is not only part of the situation but helps to define the situation. Another gap between theory and practice in the situational approach was its emphasis on the nature of the tasks at the expense of the characteristics of the leaders and followers. Clearly, the research which points out specific characteristics of leaders and followers in the way of gender-roles and sex differences illustrates this point.

We recognize that it is not reasonable to believe that individual's characteristics are unimportant and that the nature of the situation dictates all of the outcomes. Indeed, there is certainly a resurgence of interest in people who fill the leader role. The new interest on the leader in the leadership process is due in large part to the addition of sex-roles and sex differences as important elements which relate the nature of task demands and other aspects of the situation, thereby filling some unexplained facets to contemporary leadership. Rather, the most comprehensive and hence useful theories must propose an interaction among leaders, followers, and the situation.

Most lucidly, we explained the vertical dyadic linkage as a means of explaining how a leader and each follower interact in a reciprocal exchange. This recent contribution to the theory has focused more on *understanding* the process of leadership than on the outcomes produced. Recall the "in group" and "out group" terms which were introduced to explain how leader–follower influence and exchange vary within the same group. Basically, in-group members possess a close relationship with the superior. This vertical dyad enables the leader to be open to and willing to provide necessary assistance to these members.

We saw in the research related to the transactional model that there are many elements not fully explained by the situation. We decided to adopt a critical incident method to look at good and bad leadership. The assumption in that research project was to determine the general characteristics of incidents describing good and bad leadership comparing those alternative leadership descriptions and comparing the settings for reliable and stable results.

Although the critical incident studies allowed us to determine a context and a content frequency of what significant others call good or bad leadership, it also was illuminating to identify behaviors and qualities associated either with good or bad leadership that followers did *not* rank as particularly important in the setting where the behavioral episode occurred. In other words, we completed more pieces to the complex puzzle by obtaining insight about the practical use of leadership in unique group settings. These appropriate behaviors represent dimensions of leadership. However, perceptions of other behaviors were not considered as most important in that particular setting. The last group of studies involving the transactional approach to leadership explored leader sex differences, focusing on what forms of influence strategies were used by men and women to ensure followers' compliance.

Basically, we explored stereotypic values and beliefs about sex differences in male-dominant tasks. This study examined specific social power and influence processes women and men use to attain success. In one test we expected to find that males would be perceived more favorably by their followers than female leaders. Consistent with sex-role expectations, we thought that women would be receptive to upward forms of communication from followers, and male leaders would be more effective in issuing directives and other such downward forms of communications. Finally, we thought female leaders would be more likely to employ nonconfrontational influence tactics such as helpless and hinting strategies. Our results did not support these hypotheses. The leader's sex was not a variable of importance in this study, even though this study was conducted and cross-validated at two different settings. The same results were found with sex effects failing to emerge.

In essence, sex differences and gender seem to be powerful variables in *new* relationships where persons are likely to *draw from previous* values and when sex-role stereotypes are most salient. The influence of these stereotypic attitudes and beliefs wane or diffuse over time, and the characteristics and behaviors of the individual leader emerge. Proven leaders, be they male or female, enjoy support of followers, even though the followers must relinquish beliefs about the gender appropriateness of male-dominant tasks. Traits do not predict this. Behavior and style provide little insight. Even situation and contingency theories leave a gap between our understanding and the practice of leadership. No other model preceding transaction theory shows us this influence.

Furthermore, Graen (1976), a strong advocate of longitudinal research, points out that leadership is an unfolding process; it has taken time to see true, lasting patterns of relationships emerging between a leader and those who follow. Although research on the effects of leader's sex and sex-role attitudes is relatively new, much of our ability to understand and apply the influence of these contemporary variables has been through a transactional approach to leadership.

Need for More Longitudinal Studies Modelled After Project Athena

We know from our discussion of these studies that it is often inappropriate to transfer theory and practice based on male-dominated research directly to female leaders. Our book shows that it is crucial that the validity of leadership theory to practice must be based upon work which assesses female leaders. Still, there are gaps which warrant further investigation. A paramount concern is a need for more longitudinal studies, perhaps modeled after Project Athena. Such a devoted focus would do much to enhance our understanding of the developmental patterns of women as leaders. Recall, we also describe the process of leadership as a social exchange. Leader–follower relationships are reciprocal. We need to understand how various combinations of male–female interactions occur. Thus, managers want to know not only how sex differences influence leaders, but also female followers! Thus far our discussion clearly shows that there are varying patterns.

Chapter 6

Leadership Effectiveness Applications

We have discussed leadership theory and practice to help the reader to understand the underlying concepts, to review what scholarly work has been done to formulate the theories and, finally, to talk about how these theories were used in practice. Much of what was written about leadership in the way of theoretical development and testing was done before society had attempted to adapt a more egalitarian role for women in the workplace. A major contribution that this book offers is an understanding of how sex-roles or gender traits and physiological sex differences impact on the leadership process.

Now the focus is on how to apply leadership on the job. In other words, this should be a primary reference to practice leadership and, further, to offer some ideas about how to assist subordinates to perform more effectively since their performance is a reflection of one's own leadership.

HOW TO APPLY LEADERSHIP ON YOUR JOB

We are going to take the reader through the application of leadership to training and management development by calling to light many things that take place in the work environment. For example, look at your selection and placement in your organization. Undoubtedly, many things go into the screening of a candidate before he or she is chosen in a group or organization. Physical characteristics and personal traits still carry some weight in the selection process. Indeed, you may consider factors such as age, height, weight, and appearance, and social background factors such as intelligence, degree of education, and scholastic records. Also there are probably some personality inventories used to measure extroversion, self-confidence, and the like. These elements are also used in standard evaluation systems. On most forms, there are a series of traits that leaders use to evaluate their

Table 11
Common Traits Associated with Leadership

Physical Characteristics	Social Background	Intelligence
1. Age	1. Education	1. Transcripts
2. Sex	2. Social Status	2. Judgment
3. Appearance	3. Geographic birth area	3. Knowledge
4. Height		4. Creativity
5. Race		5. Scholastic Aptitude Test
6. Weight		
7. Voice		
8. Physical fitness		
9. Attractiveness		

Personality	Task-Related Characteristics	Social Characteristics
1. Aggressiveness	1. Loyalty	1. Candor
2. Alertness	2. Achievement	2. Cooperativeness
3. Dominance	3. Responsibility	3. Popularity
4. Decisiveness	4. Initiative	4. Team work
5. Extroversion	5. Persistence	5. Interpersonal Skills
6. Independence	6. Motivation	6. Tact
7. Moral courage	7. High standards	
8. Self-confidence	8. Written skills	
9. Adaptability	9. Oral skills	

followers' performance. You probably were evaluated along many of the dimensions that are illustrated in Table 11.

The important thing to remember is that research on leader traits indicates that traits and abilities required of a leader tend to vary from one situation to another. Thus, attempts to compare traits of effective and ineffective leaders have met with very limited success. The effectiveness of leadership process depends to a large extent upon the situation or environment surrounding the influence process.

Given the knowledge and skill level of particular followers, selection and placement are perhaps the most obvious methods for improving leadership performance. However, historical evidence would suggest that ability to make the best choice in selection has not been too successful (Fiedler, 1965). According to Fiedler and Chemers (1974), there is a well-worn phrase that says we must put round pegs into round holes and square pegs into square holes. This is good advice, provided that we are dealing with pegs and peg boards that do not change. But organizations do change as do leaders, and so does the relationship of the leader to the position to which he or she is assigned.

REVISING INFLUENCE ON PERSONAL TRAITS

In looking closely at Figure 2 (chapter 2), notice that the leader influence process is dynamic, and that is why we look more to a transactional approach to leadership. So, do not overrely on traits nor discount them entirely. Look at how they are used in your organization to date. Is there an overreliance on traits to make the important decisions of selection, placement, and evaluation in your group or work setting? Bear in mind that most of what was discussed in this book indicates that effective leadership does not depend upon a particular set of traits but on how well the leader's traits match the requirements of the task that he or she is facing.

Next, consider leadership styles. How do you manage your leadership styles and those of your subordinates in your organization? Clearly, the manager does more than just supervise subordinates. And you must agree that much of your effectiveness depends upon getting tasks completed through others.

In chapter 1 and 2 we reviewed bases of position power (e.g., legitimate, reward, and coercive power) and personal power (e.g., information, expert, and referent power) that seem to influence the leadership process. Ask yourself, do those who respond to me do so more because of my position bases of power or because of my personal bases of power? Is there a need to improve the blend of both? Is there an overreliance of the use of a particular power base? For example, if people comply because of the position you occupy, what might happen to your ability to influence others if the visible evidence of the source of your legitimacy was removed?

That is not to say that all managers need to rely more on personal power forms of influence. Indeed, in very structured positions, such as prison guards or wardens, a high degree of position-based influence is desired. An effective warden would be satisfied if the inmates complied, either because of the promise of rewards based upon successful action on their part (reward power) or fear of punishment bestowed by the warden's legitimate authority (coercive power).

ADAPTING ABSTRACT CONCEPTS TO PRACTICE

Aside from looking at traits, one of the things that most practicing managers get from leadership is style. Many published references describe democratic versus autocratic, participatory versus directive, relations-oriented versus task-oriented leadership styles (Glueck, 1980; Lassey, 1976; Schriescheim, 1977; Stogdill, 1977). These writers refer back to what has been already described as one of two styles: consideration versus initiation of structure.

	Initiating Structure	
Consideration	Low	High
High	low structure— high consideration	high structure— high consideration
Low	low structure— low consideration	high structure— low consideration

Figure 4.   Initiating structure and consideration.

Recall these two leadership dimensions refer to welfare for others versus concern for the work task, respectively. A graphic illustration is shown in Figure 4.

Leadership Style: The Managerial Grid.   The thing that brings these abstract leadership concepts to life is the adaptation of the two dimensions of leader behavior or style into a framework that managers can understand and use. For example, Blake and Mouton (1964, 1978) introduced what they

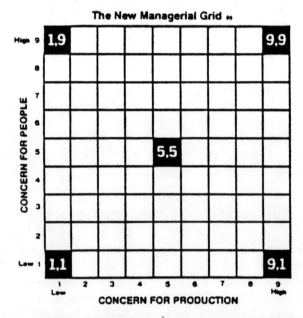

Figure 5.   The managerial grid. From *The New Managerial Grid,* by Robert R. Blake and Jane Srygley Mouton. Houston: Gulf Publishing Company, Copyright© 1978, page 11. Reproduced by permission.

describe as the "new managerial grid," and in a very simplistic way they were able to help a manager to understand his or her style in a group as well as the styles of others. This is done by training managers for a week as participant-observers in an intensive seminar. In the seminar, the participants are able to see and interpret their own behavior not as a score but rather on the basis of what it means as a direct data source from colleagues. Listed in Figure 5 is an example of the managerial grid.

The managerial grid identifies five types of managerial behavior based upon how task and employee concerns interact with each other. There are two important dimensions for labeling a leader's style—his or her concern for production and concern for people. Note, one should not be tempted to assume that the labeling simply parallels the recurrent patterns of leadership behavior that highlight initiation of structure and consideration. Blake and Mouton (1964) classify managers along these two dimensions by placing them at a particular point in a grid which is referred to by the appropriate numbers of each of the two axes ranging from 1 to 9.

For example, Style 1,1 management at the lower left of the grid is called "impoverished management" because the leader has minimal concern for either work or people. Perhaps this is also called "laissez-faire management," because the leader basically does little to influence process. Some discussion was given to this example in chapter 1 with the Lewin et al. (1939) study of Boy Scout counselors. Recall that the laissez-faire leadership condition in the Lewin et al. study amounted to a no-leadership influence condition. The same is true here; the leader does very little to influence the group process.

Style 1,9 management at the upper left-hand grid is often called "country club management," because there is an overreliance or concern for people at the expense of effectively getting the job done. The leader may be too concerned about what people think if he or she became more task-oriented. Style 9,1 located at the lower-right corner of the grid is called "authoritarian management." Here there is a strong concern for production but little regard for the people. Style 5,5 is located in the middle of the grid. This is called "middle-of-the-road management." There is a compromise between concerns for task and for people. Basically, this is a satisfying strategy doing just enough to show concern for both work and people.

Finally, Style 9,9 is located at the upper-right corner of the grid. This range is called "team and democratic management" showing a high degree of concern for both employees and production. Rather than satisfying, the 9,9 style optimizes concern for work and people. Blake and Mouton argue that the 9,9 team manager is the most effective leader because he or she can balance concerns for people and production equally.

Managers understood this more so than the empirical research that underlies how these dimension were derived. Also, managers could easily see whether there was a strong enough emphasis on work or for subordinates, given the requirements of a particular work situation. However, Blake and Mouton do not depict the grid merely as an arithmetic combination of scores. They state that the grid concept uses instrument-derived data that are made use of for applications such as conflict, initiative, and decision-making.

Be careful in interpreting this information. The grid is not a self-report scale of a person's feelings and beliefs. Clearly, the results of attitudinal feelings and behavioral acts often are different. That is, a person may make self-descriptions about being person- or relations-oriented in a job situation and behave quite differently. It is quite easy to describe one's self according to socially desirable criteria rather than in actual performance. We know that even if a manager is predisposed to desire to choose a participatory style, situational elements are strong determinants in actually changing how a manager truly will act.

Because of these problems with relying solely on style as a guide to effective leadership, we can now look at a situational perspective in our application of leadership to practice. One of the most important functions in a job may be to diagnose the many elements that have an impact on the effectiveness of one's leadership. Such a diagnosis would involve identifying and understanding the influence of factors such as individual differences of group members, including interpersonal dynamics and an increased attention to gender traits and sex differences of group members. A model of how these elements interact is found in Figure 2. Trait theories certainly point to differences in leaders. A thorough examination of the situation is another process where a leader would contemplate a particular style he or she would use. Even group structure and organizational policies and practices may be unique more to one work setting than another. For example, a group of health care professionals working under conditions of stress to save a patient's life will require a different type of leadership style than will a group of professors in a department of a university.

Although the nature of a situation may limit some generalizability, there is a likelihood that an effective leader if transferred from one group will emerge an an effective leader in another. According to Fiedler and Chemers (1974), for example, when successful or unsuccessful leaders change places, formerly ineffective groups tend to gain in performance and morale under successful leaders. On the other hand, formerly effective groups tend to decline in performance and morale under new, unsuccessful leaders. What this example speaks to is the influence of the leader as a key or hub in the leadership process. The environment in leadership typically shows the leader at the hub. The leader's followers, peers, and other elements, especially the components discussed in Figure 2 in chapter 2, make up the framework around the leader. Each environment that a leader faces will have other situational variables that are unique. Except for job demands, each of the other situational elements can be viewed with two major components: the leader's style and follower expectations. There is a reciprocal interdependence of both leaders with followers. Hence, a leader exercises influence so long as it is perceived that it is advantageous for both the leaders and the followers.

For example, if personal expectations are the perceptions of appropriate behavior for one's own role or position—the expectations define for them what they should do and what they think of others and how they should behave in certain situations. If expectations are to be compatible, then it is important to share goals and objectives. While two leaders may have different personalities because their roles require different styles, it is imperative for the organization's effectiveness that they perceive the institution's goals as their own.

Leader Style with a Contingency.   Hersey and Blanchard (1977) introduce a practitioner model which molds more leader style with a contingency. An example of their model is provided in Figure 6.

According to their practitioner model of situational leadership theory, as the level of maturity of their followers increases, leaders should begin to reduce their task behavior style and increase their relationship behavior style until the group reaches what they call a moderate level of maturity. This is shown in Figure 5 as moving from Quadrant 1 to Quadrant 2.

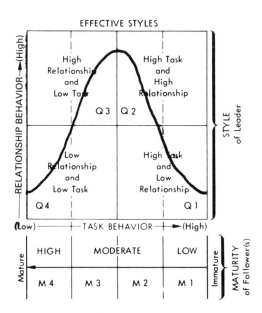

Figure 6.   Situational leadership theory. From *Management of Organizational Behavior* (3rd ed., p. 167) by P. Hersey and K. Blanchard, 1977, Englewood Cliffs, NJ: Prentice-Hall. Reprinted by permission.

Recall that leaders are not simply placing round pegs into round holes and square pegs into square holes, because the situation (the holes) changes. Anticipating such change, this practitioner model suggests that as the group moves into an above-average level of maturity, it becomes incumbent upon the leader to decrease not only task behavior style but also relationship behavior style. Why?

The maturity concept assumes that people who have a high level of maturity not only have the ability and knowledge to perform the job, but also they possess self-confidence and feel good about themselves. At this stage the followers can provide their own reinforcements; therefore, a great deal of support from the leader is no longer necessary. Further, the group views a reduction of close supervision and increase in delegation by the leader as a positive indication of trust. Thus, the leader's most effective style in quadrant four is low relationship and low task. In sum, this practitioner model attempts to simplify the contingency model (Fiedler, 1965, 1967) in such a way that the leader chooses a style that fits the appropriate situation. Unlike the contingency model, this framework suggests that the leader will adopt or change his or her style to fit the appropriate situation.

In summation, we assume that leader–follower interactions are formal relationships. There are many instances when there are supplements to leadership that reduce subordinate dependence on the leaders. For example, an employee may have experience and job expertise because he or she has worked on the job for a long time. In this case, the worker is more knowledgeable about the job requirements than most others, possibly even the supervisor. Also, many professionals such as teachers and nurses have gained knowledge from preemployment training and education. The professional employee may look to professional standards as a guide rather than to the appointed leader. Finally, rules, policies, and procedures may be so well defined and structured that there is little influence for the leader to exercise.

These supplements do not imply that leadership is not an integral management function. However, they do suggest that employees actions may be the results of factors other than the leader's behavior. As a leader of subordinates, know that to accomplish tasks, certain followers may require different rewards and punishment, and some followers respond better to one style than to another. Let us now consider the options that are open to you in the complex process involving reciprocal relationships.

THE LEADER ROLE: REWARDS AND PUNISHMENT

One of the most important aspects of a leader's role is the ability to reward and punish. The framework for the study of rewards and punishment evolves from concepts of power and motivation. If positive reward (such as merit pay, recognition, promotion) are rewarded contingent on an individual's performance, then this will serve to increase the person's motive to perform well, if he or she values the reward outcome. The administration of punishment, such as a reprimand, tends to reduce the undesired behavior. There is a relationship between leader's positive reward and subordinates' satisfaction and performance.

For example, a group of soldiers in the conduct of unit-level training may be satisfied with either the task-oriented or worker-oriented leader style during the exercise phase. However, the subsequent rewards from the leader (e.g., time off and promotion) may have the strongest impact on the workers activities and behavior. The use of negative rewards by the leader on subordinates has different effects on subordinates, depending on each individual's need level. Some authors have noted that senior employees with more than 20 years of work service have different values on retirement fringe benefits than do junior employees with less than 5 years service. As expected, the latter group prefers immediate, direct wage increases over deferred increased fringe benefits (Lawler, 1976; Szilagyi & Wallace, 1980).

Another aspect of a leader's role is proper training. Stogdill (1974) has faulted training research because the focus has been too much on the extent to which training produces attitudinal and behavorial change in the trainees. More application was demanded on its impact on the follower group. Yet, we still need to link particular training efforts with particular behavioral changes. The training may understandably increase a trainee's sensitivities; nevertheless, such increased sensitivities may be counterproductive on the job. Sensitivity training may incapacitate the leader for coping with strong opposition, threat, and challenge to the legitimacy of his or her status. What is at fault here is not the training as such, but an inadequate analysis of the changing situational demands placed on the leader.

A very important problem that has been ignored entirely concerns the effects of training on retention of the leadership role. What kind of training strengthens or weakens an individual's chances of retaining the leadership position? What experience is necessary to make an effective leader? Does one need to be trained in psychology to make an effective counselor? Does one need to be elected to be an effective leader? Finally, in many assessments of leadership training, it is impossible to determine whether the goals of the training have been met. Both the goals of training and the desired outcomes should be outlined in detail before training is conducted.

CONVERGING RELATIONSHIPS BETWEEN LEADERS, FOLLOWERS, PEERS, AND SUPERVISORS

According to Bass (1981), leader development is a continuing process. We need to understand better how experience with followers, peers, and superiors shapes one's subsequent leadership performance. The understanding of the transfer of leadership has shown that past success as a leader yields an advantage in gaining future leadership. Put simply, success breeds success. However, such an adage has special meaning for women leaders. If the nature of the task is traditionally masculine, then successful performance will be judged on masculine sex-typed behavior. Studies of women leaders will continue to increase insights on the converging relationships among leaders, followers, peers, and supervisors. Laboratory studies and one-time measurements of leadership are giving way to the type of longitudinal work in the Athena program. Because of the saliency of visibility, care needs to be taken when accepting leaders' and subordinates' cross-sex opinions and descriptions. We are convinced that organizational and leader commitment will affect positive changes over time.

At the same time, more attention has to be paid to such underlying feelings of rejection, contempt, guilt, and threat which do not surface because of superficial socialization, social desirability responses, or mistrust of the investigators. Bass (1981, p. 695) states that "it should be recognized that an effective, polite, mutual acceptance can be maintained at one level while underneath a wall of misunderstanding is maintained."

So far, the preponderance of evidence endorses the need by female members serving as leaders in majority environments to emulate the original white, male leader. However, more and more timely programs will be needed on the accommodations made by female members to the duality of their roles as both leader and token member. The dual role places unique role strains and, possibly, conflict on new female leaders, because subordinates view leaders as influential so long as leaders can facilitate satisfying followers needs.

The Linking-Pin Concept

The forcefulness of this idea can be illustrated by the "linking pin" concept developed by Likert (1961). The linking-pin concept is inextricably tied to Likert's theory of overlapping groups in organizations. An illustration of the linking pin is given in Figure 7.

Basically, the linking-pin is a person who belongs to two groups within the organization. Usually he or she is the superior in one and subordinate in the other, and it is through the vertical or hierarchical relationships that the linking-pin concept has its principal import. A typical linking-pin might be the leader of a department. He or she serves as the main link between the department and the rest of the organization. The leader is a communication link downward in serving as the channel for the flow of information on goals and objectives (such as the disseminator of policies and practices) and as the interpreter of change. Also, the leader serves as the chief channel for upward communication. Through the leader, the needs, goals, and feelings of his or her subordinates are transmitted to the upper echelons.

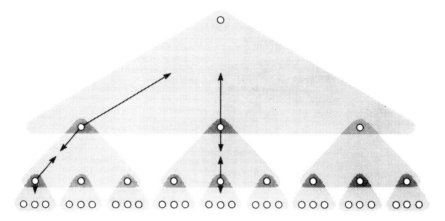

Figure 7.   The linking pin. From *New Patterns of Management* (p. 32) by R. Likert, 1961, New York: McGraw-Hill. Copyright 1961 by McGraw-Hill. Reprinted by permission.

Implications for Women

These demands are greater in early stages of leader emergence for women than for men. Why is this so? Recall that women as leaders are outgroup members in a dominant group situation. In early stages of group development, expectations about female performance in male-dominant leadership roles are biased by gender-role and sex difference stereotypes. She must dispel biased expectations that male leaders do not have to confront. For a woman to become an effective linking-pin, she must not only serve as a connector of the two levels of groups, but she must actually be a member of two groups. Thus, there are greater demands in the early stages of emergence for women, and practitioners need to be aware of this.

There are some exciting challenges facing leaders in the next two decades of this century. The emergence of reciprocal relationships and the selective attention of unique elements of sex-roles or gender traits and sex differences have greatly expanded our understanding of what takes place in the leadership process. Given our conceptual schema which unfolds a strategy for understanding leadership, the task that remains ahead is for leaders to digest and apply the findings in their work organizations.

SUMMARY

In this chapter, we have described how the process of leadership can be applied in organizational settings. We have looked at the resistant-to-change reliance on traits. There is a very active emphasis on traits for many important decisions in the workplace: selection, promotion, etc. Next, we illustrated how the simple intuitive appeal of leader style has strongly affected practitioners in leadership. The straightforward, easily measured grid is a fine practical example of style applications. The moderating influence of bases of power operationally described through systems of rewards and punishments was considered next. Leaders are reminded that the reinforcing outcomes had a significant impact on how followers complied to influence.

Next, we transposed the place of the leader, the person, at the hub of the leadership process. By viewing the leader in a pivotal manner, the practitioner could see how emerging elements, e.g., gender traits and sex differences, can impact on the leadership relationship. For example, the expectations of group members concerning the leadership abilities of men and women, as well as stereotypically masculine standards of evaluation, can influence the effectiveness of these leaders. Our aim was to underscore the fact that the applications that are made today with regard to leadership practice will exert a major influence on the long-term effectiveness of the organization's leadership in the decade to follow.

Chapter 7

Future Trends in Leadership Theory and Practice

The purpose of this final chapter is to conclude with some ideas for future work on the topic of leadership. Based on our earlier conclusions regarding contingency theory the transactional model and vertical dyadic linkage theory, we will suggest areas for future research. First to be considered are some ideas related to Stogdill's (1974) criteria for a comprehensive theory of leadership. Then some recent macroscopic trends in leadership research which deviate from the traditional, microscopic model of organizational theory will be explored. Finally, we will note some specific methodological and substantive ideas for future researchers and practitioners within both the micro and macro approaches.

Throughout this book the focus has been a traditional historical unfolding of leadership research. We have concentrated on the specific work of a particular leader with a given group of followers within a particular organizational context. This microscopic focus was chosen because it reflects the bulk of research completed to date and because it best serves the needs of the practitioner. However, as we explore future trends, we will need to go beyond a microscopic focus to a newly developing interest in macroscopic perspectives (Hunt, Sekaran, & Schriesheim, 1982).

A macroscopic perspective views leadership within a larger organizational and societal context. For example, macroscopic work suggests that the leadership process may vary in routinized, centralized organizations compared to continuous-flow, decentralized organizations (Tosi, 1982). We have ignored these broader influences on leadership as have most researchers and theorists to date. Beginning work indicates that this perspective may be fruitful, especially in clearing up some of the inconsistencies within the present, massive body of work generated thus far. But before turning to this new perspective and the promise it holds for future researchers and practitioners, let us consider some avenues for future work within the microscopic perspective we have so far followed.

A MICROSCOPIC PERSPECTIVE

Toward a Complete Theory of Leadership

In the first chapter, we said that a complete theory of leadership should explain: (a) the emergence of a leader in an unstructured group and the processes that maintain leadership, (b) the relation of leaders' personality characteristics and behaviors to group processes, and (c) the situation in which leaders' personality and behaviors are most effective (Stogdill, 1974). What will be realized is that our theories of leadership still are incomplete, even though the gap between theory and practice is decreasing (Evans, 1977; Green, 1977). A closer look at each of these three components of our hypothetically complete theory will reveal where and how future efforts of both theorists and practitioners might be directed.

Emergence and Maintenance of Leadership. Quite a bit is known about the emergence of leaders. For example, people who emerge as leaders are likely to talk a lot, be high in dominance, have the ability to accomplish the task at hand, possess valuable information, and accept group members (Bass, 1981). Given the nature of sex-role stereotypes at this time, we know that the emergent leader is likely to be a man (Megargee, 1969).

Much less is known about how leaders maintain their position. Relatedly, how do successful leaders use social power? Which types of power—reciprocal, informational, referent, expert, coercive, reward, and legitimate—are conducive to sustained leadership and in what prescribed situations? How much power should reside in the individual and how much in the position? Furthermore, does leadership go through stages of development? Are different demands placed on leaders at each of these stages? Only longitudinal studies of the leadership process will shed light on these last questions.

Personality and Group Processes. However, continued research on the relationship between leaders' personality characteristics and group performance is not encouraging. Rather, much of this work is being integrated into contingency and transactional models. For example, even the last vestiges of personality research under a contingency approach, the screen model, argues that screen factors reflect the favorability of the situation. Hence, even this has become an interactive model at its foundation.

Both contingency and transactional theories have incorporated personality theories into their general model. In the contingency model, personality characteristics of the leader are represented by his or her Least Preferred Co-worker (LPC) score. Recall that the LPC score describes a leader's style as either task- or relationship-oriented. According to Fiedler's (1964, 1967) model, groups are most effective when they are lead by someone with the

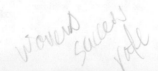

style of leadership that matches the situation's particular configuration of favorability (see Table 4 in Chapter 1). The characteristics of the leader have been placed within the general rubric of transactional theory as well. The central thesis of this model is that a leader and followers interact or transact within a given situational context (Hollander, 1978; also see Figure 1, in Chapter 1). Again, the traits of the leader per se do not remain in the theory. Rather, it is the leader's role which is important—in particular, the legitimacy of this role and how the leader is perceived by his or her constituency.

One area in which Bass (1981) feels that further research on leader's characteristics may be productive concerns the interaction of leaders' and followers' personality traits. This work may contribute insights into leader–member relations, which have been a particularly ambiguous part of contingency theory. Some research already has been conducted on different combinations of authoritarian leaders and followers (Haythorn, Couch, Haefner, Langham, & Cater, 1956) and interesting research designs in this area have been devised (Frey, 1963).

For example, one approach to understanding leader–member relations is the vertical dyadic linkage (VDL) model explored in chapter 2 (Dansereau, Graen, & Haga, 1975). In contrast to the traditional average leadership style method (ALS) which defines leader–member relations as the average of the followers' responses, the VDL model proposes that each and every follower shares an unique relationship with the leader (Dansereau, Cashman, & Graen, 1973). These multiple leader–member, dyadic linkages actually define leadership. The VDL model focuses on: (a) differences within superiors, (b) differences between individuals within work groups, and (c) the relationship between these sets of supervisory and work group differences (Dansereau, Alutto, Markham, & Dumas, 1982). One fruitful area for incorporating leaders' personalities into current research is to study leader–member relations as suggested by the VDL model.

Leaders' Effectiveness. The contemporary theories, contingency and transactional, concentrate most of their efforts on predicting under what circumstances, by whom, and with whom leadership will be most effective. This orientation necessarily helps narrow the gap between the theorist and practitioner. Fiedler's Leader-Match program is a case in point. Here the premises of contingency theory are extended to help organizations both to determine what type of leadership is called for by the specific conditions created within a work group and to accurately measure the leadership styles of candidates for the leader's position and choose among them wisely.

For example, consider an academic department at a college which is looking for an outside candidate for the position of departmental chairperson. The first step according to the contingency model would be to analyze the situational favorability of the department and place it in the appropriate octant of Table 4 (see chapter 1). Imagine that the department's members decided that the position power inherent in the role of chairperson is weak, the task structure is unclear, and leader–member relations are good. Since these are the characteristics of a moderately favorable situation, this department should recruit only high-LPC, relationship-oriented candidates. According to the model, this situation should combine with the leadership style of a high-LPC candidate to produce effective leadership.

The converse of this line of reasoning can be pursued by the candidates for this position. Knowing their LPC scores, they should uncover these three important characteristics of the situation when they interview for the position. A low-LPC, task-oriented leader would flourish in this same department, if the position power of the chair were strengthened. However, as it stands, a low-LPC person may be wary of accepting this job.

A Systems Model Approach to Leadership

Both contingency and transactional theories adopt a systems approach to examining leadership. This approach views the leader as someone ensconced in a system with multiple inputs (e.g., Bass, 1976a). These inputs include the external environment, the organization, the immediate work group, the task, the leader's behavior, and relationships between leaders and subordinates (see Figure 8).

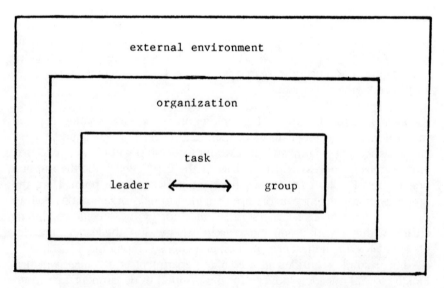

Figure 8.   The narrowing focus of research on leadership.

In Figure 8 the microscopic perspectives of contingency and transactional theories stay well within the organization, focusing mainly on the relationship between leaders and followers within a specific organizational context and directed toward accomplishment of a specific task. The macroscopic view looks at these within an overall external environment which includes other organizations and societal influences. One function of the leader is to facilitate and direct the processing of these inputs to generate outcomes—effective group performance and satisfaction. The complexity of this approach creates both methodological and substantive concerns for the systems researcher.

Designing Future Work.   When we think about avenues for future exploration of the leadership process, issues arise that reflect two conceptually distinct, but interrelated aspects of research: methodology and substance. Methodology refers to the decisions future researchers will have to make when they design projects. For example, will they conduct their study in the lab or the field, recruit both women and men as participants, and gather quantitative and/or qualitative data?

Second, our review of the literature to date suggests various ideas for the substance of these studies. The focus will be on developing testable hypotheses that build upon and expand our current understanding of the substantive issues involving leadership. Sound research always includes the consideration of both these factors, because a good idea (substance) is only useful to the extent that it is effectively defined and tested (methodology).

Methodological Issues.   One obvious methodological problem involves a dilemma between reducing this complex set of variables to a manageable size, and still remaining true to the complicated nature of the leadership process. This is related to the debate over laboratory and field designs. Lab studies boast of the control they can realize; field studies more often reflect the complexities of the real world and hence may be more applicable to actual settings.

This line of reasoning has lead Osborn and Vicars (1976) to declare that laboratory studies may exaggerate the influence of stereotypes regarding the sex-role appropriateness of leadership. The short-term, artifical nature of leadership created in the laboratory may cause subjects to rely on stereotypes to guide their responses to the leader. On the other hand, in real leader–follower relations, other experiences over time contribute to the evolution of this exchange.

Using this logic, Osborn and Vicars (1976) explain the finding that gender differences in leadership behavior occur in the lab but not in field settings as a result of exaggerated gender-role demands that arise in the lab but not in the field. In the field, actual experiences, rather than stereotypes, come to determine how the leader and followers interact. To be true to the complexities of both transactional and contingency theories, some future research needs to move into the field and use longitudinal designs such as those of Project Athena (Adams, 1979, 1980). The coordination of lab and field research would be ideal (Bass, 1981; Graen & Cashman, 1975).

There is another possible explanation for this disappearance of gender differences in leadership in the field. In the lab, subjects, typically college students, are randomly assigned to work groups and one member of the group is appointed to be the leader by the experimenter. This process of ascendancy to the position of leader is quite different from what happens in the field. Here, a man or woman who wants to be the leader attains the role either through emergence from the group or by appointment by a superior authority. This selection process may create a different transaction of leadership among leaders and followers (Hollander & Julian, 1969; Hollander & Yoder, 1980). Future research is needed to distinguish between these two competing hypotheses.

Another viewpoint on self-selection is offered by Epstein (1973). Reviewing Fogarty's (1971) *Women in Top Jobs,* Epstein concludes that the initial impetus for women's rise to the top often is catalyzed by the quirks of fate. The demands for workers during a war (Chafe, 1977), a death in the family, the need for a second income in inflationary times, and divorce are examples of life events that push women into the labor force. On the other hand, one can argue that although these circumstances may spark a woman's entry into the job market, they do not explain her rise to a leadership position (West, 1976). Furthermore, one would suspect that in the past ten years the vocational goals of women, especially college-educated women, have become more career-oriented (Bernard, 1976). Still, Epstein offers an alternative explanation about self-selection which needs to be considered by future researchers.

Transactional and contingency theories demand a complex approach to research methodology in which our view of interacting actors is expanded. At this time, both contemporary theories stress the interaction of leaders with followers. But other interactions also influence the leadership process. Leaders interact not only with followers, but also with superiors, peers, and clients.

In addition to the setting and duration studied, researchers need to think about the type of data they collect. We tend to overemphasize the value of quantitative data analysis. The complexity of the leadership process demands an expansion of our view of data as well. As noted in chapter 4, open-ended narratives used in the critical incident technique allow the practitioner to identify qualities and behaviors of the leader that are most important in a given situation. This simple, yet ingenious approach frees the participant from responding to researchers' preconceived categories, thus giving us a picture of leadership colored by all its natural richness. Greater openness to experience and clinical understanding of our data and our participants necessarily will contribute to the fullness of our understanding of the leadership process (Argyris, 1976; Bass, 1974; Cronbach, 1975).

One final methodological note concerns measurement. First, leaders' style and behavior traditionally have been measured based on an "average" score of all the followers. For example, scores from the Leader Behavior Description Questionnaire (LBDQ) generally are summed and averaged to give us an overall view of a leader's behavior. Theorists and practitioners both recognize that leaders do not treat their followers identically in a relationship. Rather, leaders often develop unique relationships with individual members of the group. For this reason, use of the vertical dyadic linkage method provides more informative and precise insights into leadership processes (Dansereau, Alutto, Markham, & Dumas, 1982).

Second, leadership has been assessed by asking leaders to describe their own style of behavior. As is true of all self-ratings, these measures are open to contamination from social desirability influences (Schriesheim & Kerr, 1974). These may reflect what leaders believe is expected of them by others rather than their actual behaviors. How often have we heard of a leader who proclaims to have an open-door policy that no one seems to use? Could the door be less open than this leader imagines? As suggested by transactional theory, research that combines the ratings of superiors, subordinates, peers, and the leaders themselves may produce a more accurate picture of leader behavior than any one of these alone.

The most fundamental measurement problems focus on our independent and dependent variables. The overriding rule of thumb of most research is to operationally define leadership effectiveness, our dependent variable, as a combination of group performance and satisfaction. But, how do we measure these? We can easily list some measurable variables, such as absenteeism, number of product units produced, and an index of self-reported job satisfaction. Even if we can quantify each of these, we still are faced with the problem of combining them (Tosi, 1982). Do we do a multivariate analysis with multiple dependent variables? Do we sum them, perhaps giving each a different weight? Questions such as these weigh heavily on the researcher.

Also, one general assumption is that we can objectively quantify aspects of group performance and satisfaction. This is a tenuous assumption. Such attempts to quantify these variables may result in a very narrow index of effectiveness which has no meaningful value (Tosi, 1982). On the other hand, broad, subjective measures of leadership effectiveness may incorporate varying, undefined conceptions of leadership and effectiveness such as sex-role biases. The result of fundamental questions such as these is a massive body of research (e.g., Bass, 1982) where conclusions are all too often amorphous. Work such as that of Nord (1977) on job satisfaction is sorely needed, or a paradigm shift within the field may be imminent (Hunt, Sekaran, & Schriesheim, 1982).

A similar line of reasoning can be projected for the independent variables of our research. Fiedler's contingency model offers the most clearly defined set of independent variables: LPC, position power, leader–member relations, and task structure. As we have seen in chapter 1, each of these can be assessed easily by completing pencil-and-paper scales. However, researchers have become increasingly disillusioned with even these variables, because uncertainties arose about how to use them. For example, with only two choices for each variable, can we be certain that a given position is weak in its power? Or does it lie somewhere in between weak and strong? Decisions such as these could change the entire picture by classifying the situation in either octants III or IV which call for different types of LPC leaders (see Appendix A). Furthermore, questions surfaced about what LPC scores validly measure, and even Fiedler fluctuated on his evaluation of the meaning of this measure (Fiedler, 1971, 1973). Again, these kinds of questions lead to a reconsideration of the foundation of leadership theory with the potential for a shift toward macroscopic analyses in the offing (Hunt & Osborn, 1982).

Substantive Issues. Historically, the study of leadership has been confined to men and college sophomores. As women (Bass, 1981; Hollander & Yoder, 1980) and minority group members fill nontraditional roles, they demand further research. Additionally, these trends call into question traditional definitions of leadership. In considering the research which continues to show that perceptions of the roles of leader and woman do not overlap much (Massengill & DiMarco, 1979; Schein, 1973), questions arise concerning our definition of leadership itself. Need this definition be restricted to stereotypic masculine roles, or could effective leadership benefit from traits we typically ascribe to women—warmth, nurturance, and helpfulness? An androgynous definition of leadership would include the positive characteristics of of both women and men (e.g., see Kaplan & Bean, 1976). Androgyny has been found to be positively related to many desirable qualities, such as intelligence and self-esteem (Spence & Helmreich, 1978). Perhaps androgynous leadership of both men and women may be more effective than the stereotypic masculine mode.

This call for an androgynous standard of leadership is strengthened by the dominant and still growing redirection of labor in this country toward service jobs. As the service sector of the job market continues to expand, the leader's role may change to fit it. It seems reasonable to expect that such service jobs will require stereotypically feminine qualities, such as nurturance and warmth, as well as the sex-typed masculine qualities traditionally associated with leadership (Schein, 1973). Again, adapting leader's and followers' expectations to a new, androgynous standard is consistent with the broader dictates of a transactional approach.

A similar, more general argument is made along these lines by human-istic, organizational theorists (e.g., Argyris, 1976). Argyris also brings interper-sonal relationships to the forefront of professional training and leadership. He argues that professional education must include two emphases simul- taneously: technical and interpersonal. Too often we have regarded technical training alone sufficient for effective management. Although Argyris recog-nizes that different tasks demand differing amounts of technical and interper-sonal skills from the leader, training must incorporate both aspects so that the effective leader is equipped to call upon both resources when the task de-mands them.

One specific research project dealing with current definitions of lead-ership would be to explore the possible role conflicts of task- and rela-tionship-oriented leadership for men and women. A task-orientation seems incompatible with feminine sex-role stereotypes. According to transactional theory, these stereotypes influence the expectations of both leaders and fol-lowers, and hence deviations of the leader from these expectations should influence group performance and satisfaction. Understanding the rela-tionship between leader's and followers' expectations would be a step toward understanding and eventually changing these expectations.

Finally, systems-based research needs to consider the broader setting in which the target group acts. For example, to understand a given work group, such as the local of a union, it is important to relate it both to the rest of the organization in which it functions and, ultimately, to society. Our current troubled economy places clear constraints on the union leader, if the constit-uency is contemplating a strike. He or she cannot work isolated from this basic economic fact. Relatedly, industrial and organizational psychologists need to remain aware of broad trends in our society, such as the continuing shift from manufacturing to service jobs (Bass, 1981). It is to this broader, macroscopic perspective that we now will turn.

A MACROSCOPIC PERSPECTIVE

Looking back to Figure 7, we can see that our focus thus far has been on the internal elements of this diagram, most notably on the relationships among the leader, followers, and their immediate situational context including the task they plan to accomplish. A macroscopic perspective does not replace this focus; rather, it expands it outward to include a wider look at the organization and external environment in which the organization operates. This change of focus is reflected in several authors' call for a "paradigm shift" (see Hunt, Sekaran, & Schriesheim, 1982). A paradigm is a general model or approach to an area of study that is shared by a scientific community and which supplies the basic assumptions under which this community functions (see Kuhn, 1962). The first point is to enumerate some aspects of the organization and the external environment that theorists project will be important in pursuing this macroscopic orientation.

Substantive Issues

According to Hunt and Osborn (1982), macroscopic factors vary along three dimensions of complexity: environmental, contextual, and structural. Environmental variables can be further subdivided into two components: general and specific. General environmental factors refer to broad, societal influences, such as education or the socialization process, economic pressures, legal–political regulations, and so on. For example, the format of education can be related to the needs of our industrialized society on both technological and sociocultural grounds (for consideration of the latter, see Bowles & Gintis, 1976). As each of these changes over time, its effects will be felt on the organization and hence on both leaders and followers. Our previous hypothesis about society-wide changes in sex-role stereotypes is a case in point.

The specific environmental complexities faced by an organization include its relations with other organizations. For example, the most recent trend is for multinational corporations to expand into unrelated ventures; 60% of total assets held by manufacturing corporations in this country in 1980 are controlled by the top 200 companies (*Statistical Abstracts,* 1981, p. 541). This aggregation of resources must affect the way organizations relate to each other within a a competitive marketplace.

Contextual and structural complexities both deal with intraorganizational factors. Contextual complexity comprises the size of the organization, the intricacy of turning raw materials into finished products (technological sophistication), and the variety of duties performed by different employees (technological variability). Structural complexity involves the basic characteristics of the organization: its degree of formalization, whether or not it is hierarchically arranged, the amount of impersonal control, and so on.

Finally, Hunt and Osborn (1982) expand our traditional view of leadership to include both vertical and lateral leadership (see Sayles, 1964). We generally regard leadership as vertical by emphasizing the relations of a manager with both his or her subordinates and superiors. However, leaders also operate laterally when they develop guidelines for interunit exchanges, structure relations with their colleagues, and respond to peer pressures. Little is known about lateral leadership, so this concept opens new doors for exploration.

Another developing trend in the definition of leadership itself is to distinguish between managerial or supervisory (transactional) leadership and charismatic (transformational) leadership. Transactional leaders are those who "approach followers with an eye to exchanging one thing for another:

jobs for votes, or subsidies for campaign contributions. Such transactions comprise the bulk of the relationships among leaders and followers, especially in groups, legislatures, and parties" (Burns, 1978, p. 3). A transformational (Bass, 1982) or charismatic (Tosi, 1982) leader, on the other hand, seeks to inspire followers to sacrifice to attain superordinate goals. Gandhi, Churchill, and even Hitler reflect this second type of leadership. Clearly, these are radically different types of leaders involving qualitatively distinct approaches to leading. Our bias, and one which has been shared by many researchers to date, is to study managing, which we must recognize as only one potential form of leadership.

Expanding our substantive view of leadership to include both macro- and microscopic perspectives as illustrated in Figure 7 opens up linkages to more general theoretical bases within the social sciences (Hunt & Osborn, 1982). Reinforcement (Skinner, 1974) and exchange (Homans, 1961) theories may suggest areas for future work involving environmental contingencies. For example, governmental deregulations may reward new organizational strategies, such as advertising and rate specials among the airlines. These new ventures, in turn, will call for different patterns of effective leadership behavior. As the president of Chrysler Corporation, Lee Iacocca exemplified this change in leadership style in response to economic demands.

At a macroscopic level, attribution theory (Kelley, 1973) may offer insights into leader–member relations. Attribution theory deals with people's perceptions of their own and other people's behavior. For example, if a worker fails to finish a specific task on time, an outsider may attribute this failure to conditions outside him- or herself, such as the late arrival of a central piece of equipment. Having these two discrepant perceptions could potentially damage the relationship between this actor and observer (the leader). Attribution theory may proffer some suggestions for bringing these perceptions together and hence improve leader–member relations. Such an approach would be consistent with the notions of transaction between leaders and followers, discussed in chapters 1 and 2 (Hollander, 1978).

As we can see, both macro- and microscopic perspectives are compatible, and they offer us an expanded view of leadership not taken to date. This addition of organizational and societal elements to the leadership equation holds out the promise of better predictability to both the researcher and the practitioner. The expanded opportunities for future research generated by such an enlarged position are exciting and challenging.

Methodological Issues

The most obvious methodological point concerns the expanded set of independent variables to be considered by researchers. The basic factors well-substantiated by microscopic researchers (e.g., the impact of leader' consideration and initiation of structure) need to be entered first into our regression equation. Then, organizational and societal factors need to be added so that their contributions over and above what researchers already know can be assessed. Finally, more fine-tuned work needs to consider the interaction of variables from each level of our organizational analysis.

One way to enhance the predictability of our regression models is to engage in more systematic programs of research, such as our work on Project Athena. Here, we followed the same individuals through four years of leadership training and experiences within the same controlled environment. Our findings crossed several different techniques of data collection, ranging from laboratory experiments to surveys, interviews, and observations. The richness of these data let us compare findings from one setting and using one technique to other different settings and procedures. Programmatic research such as this will help ferret out short-term, artificial findings from long-term, replicable results.

Finally, this expanded model of leadership argues for a more dynamic approach to studying and understanding leadership processes. For example, do leaders pass through varying stages of leadership? Argyris (1976) asks: Are these stages influenced not only by altering leader–member relations, but also by fluctuations in the broader picture, such as economic changes? An entire new series of questions regarding phases of leadership is suggested by this enlarged perspective.

Conclusion. Recent innovations in leadership theory suggest that future research concentrate on an expanded model of leadership processes diagrammed in Figure 8. The actual exchange between a leader and followers is embedded in an expanding series of situational factors which include the task, the organization and the external environment. It is expected that more predictive models of leadership will emerge from programmatic research that involves variables representative of each of these micro- and macroscopic levels of the situational context. Although present findings concerning leadership are often inconclusive, the expanded perspective presented here offers promise for future researchers and practitioners alike. Well-entrenched in the lessons of the past, we are ready to tackle the challenges of the future, and enlarged models such as this have paved the way for us to begin.

Leadership Practice

Moreover, the gap between the practitioner and theorist is narrowing. This is the result of two interrelated trends: (a) the practice of leadership as exemplified by industrial/organizational psychologists and personnel administrators is becoming less of an art and more of a science; and (b) academic researchers are assuming the roles of becoming and training program evaluators.

The former is realized in the eclectic nature of this book. Theory and practice are discussed in terms familiar to both parties. Research is moving into the field, and the field, in turn, is pointing out areas to be studied. Additionally, theory is being translated into practice. For example, a practitioner guided by contingency theory can assess the leadership style of managerial candidates as well as the favorability of the situation toward these leadership styles.

Program evaluators are collecting data and making policy recommendations. These were two of the functions of the work on Project Athena. These evaluators ask questions concerning the replacement and succession of leaders, leadership maintenance, effective leadership, and the evolving definition of leadership.

For example, West Point policymakers have asked researchers to examine the strengths and difficulties of female cadets since a year before their arrival in 1976. Our work has come to several unanticipated conclusions that have helped these policymakers to better assimilate women into the Corps of Cadets. This work spanned every aspect of cadets' lives from physical training to social interactions. Regarding physical training, we found that the inability of some women to complete runs within the time period allotted their group reflected negatively and persistently on the women's leadership ratings (Rice, Yoder, Adams, Priest, & Prince, 1984). Both of these pieces of research and others from equally divergent settings have helped guide policymakers through the previously uncharted waters of a coeducational Academy.

One area in which practitioners need to make serious decisions about leadership is in advising policymakers. To improve leadership effectiveness, practitioners can recommend three courses of action: (a) choose leaders who best "fit" the existent situation, (b) change people (training), and/or (c) change the situation.

As we have seen, Fiedler's contingency model argues that training leaders is dysfunctional. Rather, he posits that policymakers should establish procedures whereby leaders can be selected who best match the existent situation. Some changes in the situation may be possible; for example, one could enhance or diminish the position (legitimate) power of the leader. Clearly, the focus here is on securing the best fit of the leader, with situational changes made only if necessary.

This approach may not be feasible or ethical in light of affirmative action laws. For example, if the leader's role continues to be regarded as a masculine one, then the leader who will best fit the situation always is a man. The result is the perpetuation of discriminatory hiring practices. Seeking the best fit is one way to keep leadership as it is, rather than viewing it as a process that should be scrutinized and improved upon whenever possible.

Much effort has been expended in the area of training. There has been a boom in training programs from sensitivity training to assertiveness training (Morton & Bass, 1964) and role playing (Moreno, 1955). However, a growing body of evidence suggests that training, especially if it is not reinforced and sustained in the work setting, is not effective in positively altering employees' attitudes and behaviors (e.g., Bowers, 1973; Bunker, 1965; House, 1968; Oshry & Harrison, 1966). Furthermore, such training has been criticized on ethical grounds for imposing trainers' values on recipients (Lakin, 1969). Finally, human process training and developmental interventions have not been linked directly to improvements in productivity (Adams, 1977).

A more situation-centered approach, such as that adopted at West Point in our analysis of tokenism and situational changes, may be more realistic and effective. Furthermore, this situational perspective is consistent with the recent insurgence of a macroscopic perspective on leadership. By structuring the situation to encourage positive leadership, this type of behavior often results. At West Point, institutional policies—admitting more women, outlawing anti-female expressions and reassessing standards of evaluation—all contributed to a reduction in the situationally created inhibitions of tokenism. Changing these policies was much easier, more ethical, and more realistic than trying to fit women into a role that epitomized masculinity.

CONCLUSION

In this book, our goal has been to explore the dynamics of effective leadership for women and men. We started with a historical overview of research and theory on leadership ending with two contemporary, interactive models: contingency and transactional. The second chapter expanded on this latter viewpoint by considering leadership as an influence process. Here, we introduced the vertical dyadic linkage model for assessing leadership processes and further explored the sex-role literature pertinent to a contemporary analysis of leadership. In the next two chapters, we presented an example of systematic, programmatic research conducted with male and female cadets at the U.S. Military Academy at West Point. The longitudinal nature of this project, the control and consistency afforded by this setting, comparisons of men and women in similar leadership positions, and the richness of the data set allowed us to present a look at the dynamics of leadership that generally is unavailable to the researcher.

However, we were not content with a simple pedagogical review. In the next two chapters, we synthesized this work with current theories with an eye to making pragmatic suggestions for practitioners. As the West Point project was undertaken to combine academic understandings with the need to apply our findings to a real-life setting, this book was designed to do the same. This integration of the academic literature with the needs of practitioners culminated in chapters 5 and 6. Finally, in chapter 7 we noted some exciting and challenging areas for future work by both researchers and practitioners which call for extensions of our work to include women and minority group members as well as macroscopic situational influences. The continued exchange of resources between academic and applied settings can only serve to further enhance our understanding of this evasive but influential phenomenon—leadership.

Appendix A*

High- and Low-LPC Leaders Juxtaposed on Group-Task Situations

VERY FAVORABLE GROUP SITUATIONS (OCTANTS I AND II)

High-LPC Leaders

The high-LPC person tends to be self-oriented, in the sense of being concerned with gaining personal recognition and being considered successful as a person (Bass et al., 1965). He or she can gain this personal recognition and reward without too much difficulty in a situation in which the person is accepted and liked by the group, in which the individual occupies a powerful position, and in which he or she is in control of the task. Just being liked or accepted and being powerful provide most of the need satisfaction the high-LPC leader seeks. Therefore, the leader experiences no particular threat, and has little need to control the interpersonal relations which already give him or her what is desired. The leader does not have to exert oneself either to obtain a good relationship or to perform well on the task. The leader can rest on his or her laurels and remain relatively passive, nondirective, permissive.

Low-LPC Leaders

The situation in which the group accepts the leader and in which the leader has power and a clearly structured task is excellently suited for the leadership style of the low-LPC person. The leader does not have to worry about relationship with group members since the leader feels accepted, and has all the influence needed to perform the task. Since the leader gains satisfaction from the task, the leader will, with minimal apparent effort, direct and coordinate the task-relevant aspects of the group situation. Being less concerned with feelings of the group members, the low-LPC leader is also less likely to have conflicts or misgivings about managing and directing the group. Since the task is structured and the leader knows what to do and how to do it, he or she will feel justified in rejecting and punishing those who would hinder the leader in getting the job done (see, for example, Hawkins, 1962). Therefore, the low-LPC leader is also likely to be successful in directing the group task.

---

*From *A Theory of Leadership Effectiveness* (pp. 183–185) by F. E. Fiedler, 1967, New York: McGraw Hill. Copyright 1982 by McGraw Hill Publishers. Reprinted with permission.

SOMEWHAT UNFAVORABLE GROUP SITUATIONS (OCTANTS IV AND V)

High-LPC Leaders

As the favorableness of the situation decreases, so, by definition, will the leader's ability to influence and control the group. Hence the leader will sense somewhat greater difficulty in gaining the rewards and recognition which are sought. The leader may not be well accepted by the group, the task may be vague and unstructured, or the leader's position may be weak. One consequence of this less favorable situation will be an effort on the part of the relationship-oriented, high-LPC leader to interact more intensively with the members of the group. Wishing to be known as a good person, the leader will become somewhat more concerned with the feelings and opinions of group members, hence more highly rated in consideration. The leader will become more responsive to the group, more permissive in interactions, and more relationship-oriented.

This type of behavior is, of course, quite appropriate for chairpersons of committees or leaders of creative groups falling into Octant IV. These must utilize and exploit the intelligence and creativity of the group members in order to be successful. It would also be appropriate for groups in which the task is structured but the leader is only moderately well accepted. Here the conciliatory, permissive, considerate leader who allows members a voice in the task and encourages member participation is more likely to get results than one who is impatient with the group.

Low-LPC Leaders

In the somewhat more difficult situation (Octant IV) in which the task is less well structured, in which the leader's power is limited, or in which the group does not fully accept the leader (Octant V), the low-LPC person, like the high-LPC counterpart, is likely to become somewhat threatened. However, being task-oriented, the leader will become more tense and concerned about the task and hence more impatient to get it done. Since the task in Octant IV situations is unstructured and vague, the impatience to get on with the task will tend to cut off group discussion. The lesser concern for the feelings of the group members will inhibit them from free discussion of the problem and from venturing new and offbeat ideas. As a result, the leader will be unable to make full use of his group members, and the group productivity will suffer. In Octant V situations (in which the leader has position power, the task is highly structured, but the leader is not too well accepted) the low-LPC leader's behavior and attitudes are likely to alienate the members of the group and so reduce their motivation to work.

RELATIVELY UNFAVORABLE SITUATIONS (OCTANTS VIII AND VIII-A)

High-LPC Leaders

The style of the high-LPC leader will be less successful in situations in which the leader enjoys relatively little control. Here the members may be somewhat anxious, and therefore, less concerned with the task; the group may become less cohesive, and the leader's weak position power will no longer suffice to keep the members in line. The leader is likely to become quite threatened in these circumstances, and therefore, will tend to increase the rate and intensity of interactions with members in an effort to maintain control over the group processes so that the leader can be assured about the recognition and rewards which are sought. The anxiety may well lead to dysfunctional interactions with group members. The leader may become demanding, dictatorial, and testy. To a correspondingly lesser degree, the leader will attend to the task-relevant aspects of the group situation.

Low-LPC Leaders

The leader who describes a least preferred co-worker in very unfavorable terms tries to obtain satisfaction and social reinforcement through involvement with the task. As Bishop's (1964) study has shown, the leader tends to experience an increase in self-esteem and adjustment if one feels that he or she has succeeded in the task, whether or not interpersonal relations have been successful. Therefore, in trying to control the situation, low-LPC leaders tend to become more task-oriented in group situations which are unfavorable. It is more important to them that the task be well done than that the group members be satisfied and enjoy good relations with the leader.

Very unfavorable situations do not allow the leader to exert much influence over the group, and the low-LPC person, like the high-LPC counterpart, will perceive a threat to need satisfaction. However, the low-LPC person's needs are gratified by success in the performance of the task. Therefore, the leader will become more and more involved in activities related to the task and less in interpersonal relations with group members. The leader will attempt to control task-relevant aspects of the group situation in order to compensate for the threat. Groups under more stressful or threatening conditions tend to be more tolerant of directive, even inconsiderate, leadership (cf. S. L. A. Marshall, 1959) which channels their activities into task-relevant behavior. Therefore, group members are more likely to work effectively with task-oriented leaders than with leaders who are primarily concerned with their own status or with good interpersonal relations.

Coding Categories For Critical Incidents of Good and Bad Leadership[1]

1.	Expertise:	Leader did or did not possess special knowledge or skill.
	Good:	S/he had all the facts and knew what s/he was talking about.
	Bad:	S/he did not have the facts, and did not know what s/he was talking about.
2.	Motivates:	Leader did or did not motivate, encourage, or inspire subordinates to put forth a high level of effort.
	Good:	S/he motivated and cheered us on.
	Bad:	S/he failed to motivate or inspire us.
3.	Cohesiveness:	Leader did or did not instill cohesiveness or unity.
	Good:	S/he brought us all closer together as a group and a team.
	Bad:	S/he was unable to coordinate our efforts for good teamwork.
4.	Role Model:	Leader did or did not influence subordinates by example.
	Good:	S/he always set an example by his/her personal appearance and conduct.
	Bad:	S/he expected us to be properly attired, but s/he usually was not.
5.	Involvement:	Leader actions did or did not reflect personal concern and interest in subordinates' well-being.

---

[1]If a good leadership trait, quality, or action is described as a part of a bad leadership critical incident (or vice versa), it is not coded.

	Good:	S/he always checked our feet for blisters and made sure we were taken care of.
	Bad:	S/he was indifferent to us, and did not give cadets help when they needed it.
6.	Contingent Sanctions:	Leader rewards/punishes subordinates as a result of subordinate actions.
	Good:	S/he said s/he was proud of our unit's performance.
	Bad:	S/he made us do extra marching practice because of our poor marching performance.

(This category also includes leaders acting excessively in response to a specific plebe action, either through additional harassment or by overrewarding or overpunishing subordinate actions.)

7.	Noncontingent Sanctions:	Leader administers rewards/punishments to subordinate without provocation in terms of subordinate actions.
	Good:	S/he arranged for us all to get ice cream for no specific reason.
	Bad:	S/he harassed the plebe just for the fun of it.

(This category also includes incidents in which the initial harassment, which was unprovoked by a specific incident, led to the plebe making a mistake, followed by additional harassment.)

8.	Fairness:	Leader did or did not treat subordinates similarly.
	Good:	S/he did not have favorites.
	Bad:	S/he harassed him because he had had prior service.

(Fairness is determined not by coder's subjective appraisal of the situation but rather because the respondent stated why the leader's actions toward a plebe were fair/unfair.)

9.	Responsibility:	Leader did or did not take responsibility for his/her actions.
	Good:	S/he admitted that s/he had made a mistake.
	Bad:	S/he blamed others for something that was really his/her fault.

10. Downward Communication: Leader did or did not inform subordinates of the rules, duties, goals, and rationale behind various policies.

                    Good: S/he met with the squad beforehand to tell us what to expect.

                    Bad: S/he never explained why or how certain duties were performed.

11. Upward Communication: Leader did or did not allow subordinates to ask questions, discuss or relate information to him/her.

                    Good: S/he always encouraged us to ask questions and listened carefully to our ideas.

                    Bad: S/he never allowed us to explain or ask clarifying questions.

12.   Organizes: Leader did or did not organize, structure, or coordinate activities.

                    Good: S/he arranged it so that the equipment was rotated through the squad.

                    Bad: S/he had no idea what the training activities were for the day.

13.   Other: Please write on the response sheet a brief description of the incident.

REFERENCES

Adams, J. (1977). *An evaluation of organizational effectiveness.* Unpublished doctoral dissertation, Purdue University, West Lafayette, IN.

Adams, J. (1979, June). *Report of the admission of women to the U.S. Military Academy, Project Athena, III.* West Point, NY: U.S. Military Academy.

Adams, J. (1980, June). *Report of the admission of women to the U.S. Miltary Academy, Project Athena, IV.* West Point, NY: U.S. Military Academy.

Adams, J., & Hicks, J. M. (1978, November). *Leader sex, leader descriptions of own behavior and subordinates description of leader behavior.* Paper presented at Military Testing Association Conference, Oklahoma City, OK.

Adams, J. & Hicks, J. M. (1981, November). *Leadership performance appraisal ratings during cadet field training.* Paper presented at Military Testing Association Conference, Washington, DC.

Adams, J., Priest, R. F., & Prince, H. T. II. (in press). Achievement motive: Analyzing the validity of the wofo. *Psychology of Women Quarterly.*

Adams, J., Priest, R. F., Rice, R. W., & Prince, H. T., II. (1980, October). *Effects of rater attitudes and attributes on female and male leader's effectiveness.* Paper presented at the 1980 Biannual AMEDD Psychology Symposium, Washington.

Adams, J., Prince, H. T., Yoder, J. D., & Rice, R. W. (1981). Group performance at West Point. *Armed Forces and Society, 7,* 246–255.

Adams, J., Rice, R. W., & Instone, D. (1984, Summer). Critical incidents of good and bad leadership. *Armed Forces and Society, 10,* 597–611.

Adams, J., Rice, R. W., Instone, D., & Prince, H. T. II. (1980). *The 1979 summer leadership study: Procedures and descriptive analyses for the basic questionnaire* (Technical Report, 80-1). West Point, NY: AG Printing Office.

Adams, J. S. Inequity in social exchange. (1965). In L. Berkowitz (Ed.), *Advances in experimental social psychology* (Vol. 2). New York: Academic Press.

Allen, E. J. (1979). Faculty in the 80s: Diversity and reorientation. *Trends 2000, 1(3),* 10.

Alvarez, R. (1968). Informal reactions to deviance in simulated work organizations. *American Sociological Review, 33,* 895–912.

Angrist, S. S. & Almquist, E. (1975). *Careers and contingencies: How college women juggle with gender.* New York: Dunellen.

Argyris, C. (1976). *Increasing leadership effectiveness.* New York: Wiley.

Aronson, E., Blaney, N., Sikes, J., Stephen, C. & Snapp, M. (1975). Busing and racial tension: The jigsaw route to learning and liking. *Psychology Today, 8,* 43–50.

Ashour, A. S. (1973). The contingency model of leadership effectiveness: An evaluation. *Organizational Behavior and Human Performance, 9,* 339–355.

Ayers-Nachamkin, B., Cann, C. H., Reed, R., & Horne, A. (1982). Sex and ethnic differences in the use of power. *Journal of Applied Psychology, 67,* 464–471.

Bales, R. F., & Slater, P. E. (1955). Role differentiation in small decision-making groups. In T. Parsons, (Ed.), *Family socialization, and interaction process.* Glencoe, IL: Free Press.

Bandura, A. (1962). Social learning through imitation. In M. R. Jones (Ed.), *Nebraska symposium on motivation* (Vol. 10). Lincoln, NE: University of Nebraska Press.

Bartol, K. M. (1978). The sex structuring of organization: A search for possible causes. *Academy of Management Review, 3,* 805–815.

Bass, B. M. (1960). *Leadership, psychology, & organizational behavior.* New York: Harper.

Bass, B. M. (1974). The substance and the shadow. *American Psychologist, 29,* 870–886.

Bass, B. M. (1976a). A system survey research feedback for management and organizational development. *Journal of Applied Behavior Science, 12,* 215–229.

Bass, B. M. (1976b). Some observations about a general theory of leadership and interpersonal behavior, In W. R. Lassey & R. R. Fernandez, (Eds.), *Leadership and social exchange,* (2nd ed. pp. 66–70). La Jolla, CA: University Associates,

Bass, B. M. (1977). Utility of managerial self-planning on a simulated production task with replication in twelve countries. *Journal of Applied Psychology, 62,* 506–509.

Bass, B. M. (1981). *Stogdill's handbook of leadership* (rev. ed.). New York: Macmillan.

Bass, B. M. (1982). Intensity of relation, dyadic-group considerations, cognitive categorization, and transformational leadership. In J. G. Hunt, U. Sekaran, & C. A. Schriesheim (Eds.), *Leadership: Beyond establishment views.* Carbondale, IL: Southern Illinois University Press.

Bass, B. M., & Dunteman, G. (1963). Behavior in groups as a function of self, interaction, and task orientation. *Journal of Abnormal and Social Psychology, 66,* 419–428.

Bass, B. M., McGehee, C. R., Hawkins, W. C., Young, P. C., & Gebel, A. S. (1953). Personality variables related to leaderless group discussion behavior. *Journal of Abnormal Social Psychology, 48,* 120–128.

Bell, G. B. (1967). Determinants of span of control. *American Journal of Sociology, 73,* 100–109.

Bem, S. L. (1977). *The bem sex-role inventory.* La Jolla, CA: University Associates.

Bender, L. R. (1979, August). *Women as leaders: The impact of leader attributes of masculinity and femininity and of follower attributes toward women.* Unpublished doctoral dissertation, Buffalo, S.U.N.Y., 12–24.

Bennis, W. K. (1976). Post-Bureaucratic Leadership. In W. R. Lassey & R. R. Fernandez (Eds.). *Leadership and social exchange* (2nd ed.), (pp. 180–184). La Jolla, CA: University Associates.

Bernard, J. (1976). Change and stability in sex-role norms and behaviors. *Journal of Social Issues, 32,* 207–224.

Besco, R. O., & Lawshe, C. H. (1959). Foreman leadership as perceived by superiors and subordinates. *Personnel Psychology, 12,* 573–582.

Birnbaum, J. A. (1975). Life patterns and self-esteem in gifted family oriented and career committed women. In M. T. S. Mednick, S. S. Tangi, & L. W. Hoffman (Eds.), *Women and achievement: Social and motivated analyses.* Washington, DC: Hemisphere.

Blades, J. W., & Fiedler, F. E. (1973, January). *Participative management, member, intelligence, and group performance* (Tech. Rp. 73-40). Seattle, WA: University of Washington, Organizational Research.

Blake, R. R., & Mouton, J. S. (1962a). The intergroup dynamics of win-lose conflict and problem-solving collaboration in union-management relations. In M. Sherif (Ed.), *Intergroup relations and leadership.* New York: Wiley.

Blake, R. R., & Mouton, J. S. (1962b). Overevaluation of own group's product in intergroup competition. *Journal of Abnormal and Social Psychology, 62,* 237–238.

Blake, R. R., & Mouton, J. S. (1964). *The managerial grid.* Houston, TX: Gulf.

Blake, R. R., & Mouton, J. S. (1978). *The new managerial grid.* Houston, TX: Gulf.

Blake, R. R., Mouton, J. S., & Sloma, R. L. (1964). The union management intergroup laboratory: strategy for resolving intergroup conflict, *Journal of Applied Behavioral Sciences, 1,* 25–27.

Blau, P. M. & Scott, W. R. (1962). *Formal organizations.* San Francisco, CA: Chandler.

Bowers, D. G. (1973). OD techniques and their results in 23 organizations: The Michigan ICL study. *Journal of Applied Behavior Science, 9,* 21–43.

Bowers, D. G., & Seashore, S. E. (1966). Predicting organizational effectiveness with a four factor theory of leadership. *Administrative Science Quarterly, 11,* 238–263.

Bowles, S., & Gintis, H. (1976). *Schooling in capitalist America.* New York: Basic.

Bowman, G. W., Worthy, N. B., & Greyser, S. A. (1965). Are women executives people? *Harvard Business Review, 43,* 14–28.

Brenner, M. M. (1970, September). *Management development activities for women.* Paper presented at the American Psychological Association Convention, Miami, FL.

Broverman, I., Vogel, S. R., Broverman, D. M., Clarkson, F. E., & Rosenkrantz, P. S. (1972). Sex-role stereotypes: A current appraisal. *Journal of Social Issues, 28,* 59–78.

Bryson, J., & Kelley, G. (1978). A political perspective in leadership emergence, stability, and change in organizational networks. *Academy of Management Review, 3,* 712–723.

Bunker, D. R. (1965). Individual applications of laboratory training. *Journal of Applied Behavioral Science, 1,* 131–148.

Burns, W. (1978). *Leadership.* New York: McGraw-Hill.

Butterfield, D. A., & Bartol, K. M. (1977). Evaluators of leader behavior: A missing element in leadership theory In J. G. Hunt & L. L. Larson (Eds.), *Leadership: The cutting edge.* (167–188). Carbondale, IL: Southern Illinois University Press.

Butterfield, D. A., & Powell, G. N. (1981). Effect of group performance, leader sex, and rater sex on ratings of leader behavior. *Organizational Behavior and Human Performance, 28,* 129–141.

Calvin, A. D., Hoffmann, F. K., & Harden, E. D. (1957). The effects of intelligence and social atmosphere on group problem-solving behavior. *Journal of Social Psychology, 45,* 61–74.

Campbell, J. P., Dunnette, M. D., Lawler, E. E., & Weick, K. E. (1970). *Managerial behavior, performance, and effectiveness.* New York: McGraw-Hill.

Canter, R. J. (1975). Achievement-related expectations and aspirations in college women. *Sex Roles, 5,* 543–570.

Carey, A. (1967). The hawthorne studies: A radical criticism. *American Sociological Review, 32,* 425–36.

Carter, L. F., Haythorn, W., & Howell, M. A. (1950). A further investigation of the criteria of leadership. *Journal of Abnormal and Social Psychology, 45,* 358–368.

Cartwright, D. (1965). Influence, leadership, control, In J. G. Marsh, (Ed.), *Handbook of organizations.* Chicago, IL: Rand McNally.

Carzo, R., & Yanouzas, J. N. (1969). Effects of flat and tall organization structure. *Administrative Science Quarterly, 14,* 178–191.

Chafe, W. H. (1977). *Women and equality: Changing patterns in American culture.* New York: Oxford University Press.

Chemers, M. M., & Skrzypek, G. J. (1972). Experimental test of the contingency model of leadership effectiveness. *Journal of Personality and Social Psychology, 24,* 172–177.

Cherry, F., & Deaux, K. (1978). Fear of success vs. fear of gender-inappropriate behavior. *Sex Roles, 4,* 97–102.

Coch, L., & French, J. R. P. (1948). Overcoming resistance to change. *Human Relations, 1,* 512–32.

Cohen, E., & Burns, P. (1978, May). *SPSS-manova-multivariate analysis of variance and covariance.* Evanston, IL: Vogel Computing Center, Northwestern University.

Cook, S. W. (1971, August). *The effect of unintended racial contact upon racial interaction and attitude change* (Final report, projects No. 5-1320, contract no. OEC-4-7-051320-0273). Washington, DC: U.S. Office of Education, Bureau of Research.

Cronbach, L. J. (1951). Coefficient alpha and the internal structure of tests. *Psychometrics, 16,* 297–334.

Cronbach, L. J. (1975). Beyond the two disciplines of scientific psychology. *American Psychologist, 30,* 116–127.

Dansereau, F., Alutto, J. A., Markham, S. E. & Dumas, M. (1982). Multiplexed supervision and leadership: an application of within and between analysis. In J. G. Hunt, U. Sekaran, & C. A. Schriesheim (Eds.), *Leadership: Beyond establishment views.* Carbondale, IL: Southern Illinois University Press.

Dansereau, F., Cashman, J. & Graen, G. (1973). Instrumentality theory and equity theory as complementary approaches in predicting the relationship of leadership and turnover among managers. *Organizational Behavior and Human Performance, 13,* 46–78.

Dansereau, F., Graen, G., & Haga, W. J. (1975). A vertical dyad linkage approach to leadership within formal organizations: A longitudinal investigation of the role making process. *Organizational Behavior and Human Performance, 13,* 46–78.

Darley, S. (1976). Big time careers for the little woman: A dual-role dilemma. *The Journal of Social Issues, 32,* 85–98.

Davis, L., & Cherns, A. B. (Eds.). (1975). *The quality of working life.* New York: Free Press.

Deaux, K. (1972). To err is humanizing: But sex makes a difference. *Representative Research in Social Psychology, 3,* 20–28.

Deaux, K. (1976a). *The behavior of women and men.* Monterey, CA: Brooks/Cole.

Deaux, K. (1976b). Sex: A perspective on the attribution process. In O. J. Harvey, T. Ickes, & R. F. Kidd (Eds.), *New directions in attribution research* (Vol. 1). Hillsdale, NJ: Lawrence Erlbaum.

Deaux, K. & Emswiller, T. (1974). Explanations of successful performance of sex-linked tasks: what is skill for the male is luck for the female. *Journal of Personality and Social Psychology, 29,* 80–85.

Deutsch, M., & Collins, M. (1951). *Interracial housing: a psychological evaluation of a social experiment.* Minneapolis, MN: University of Minnesota Press.

Dubin, R. (1951). *Human relations in administration, the sociology of organizations: readings and cases.* New York: Prentice Hall.

Ellis, J., & Moore, R. (1974). *School for soldiers,* New York: Oxford Press.

Epstein, C. F. (1973). Review of Fogarty et al., Women in top jobs. *Social Forces, 52,* 288.

Eskilson, A., & Wiley, M. G. (1979). Sex composition and leadership in small groups. *Sociometry, 39,* 183–194.

Evans, M. G. (1977). Commentary on the state of the field and some neglected issues. In J. G. Hunt & L. L. Larson (Eds.), *Leadership: The cutting edge* (109–115). Carbondale, IL: Southern Illinois University Press.

Farrow, D. L., Valenzi, E. R., & Bass, B. M. (1980). A comparison of leadership and situational characteristics within profit and nonprofit organizations. *Proceedings of the Academy of Management,* Detroit, MI.

Festinger, L. (1954). A theory of social comparison processes. *Human Relations, 1,* 117–140.

Festinger, L. (1957). *A theory of cognitive dissonance,* Stanford, CA: Stanford University Press.

Fiedler, F. E. (1964). A contingency model of leadership effectiveness. In L. Berkowitz (Ed.), *Advances in experimental social psychology.* New York: Academic Press.

Fiedler, F. E. (1965). Engineering the job to fit the manager. *Harvard Business Review, 43,* 115–122.

Fiedler, F. E. (1966). The effect of leadership and cultural heterogenity on group performance: A test of the contingency model. *Journal of Experimental Social Psychology, 2,* 237–264.

Fiedler, F. E. (1967). *A theory of leadership effectiveness.* New York: McGraw-Hill.

Fiedler, F. E. (1971). Validation and extension of the contingency model of leadership effectiveness: a review of empirical findings. *Psychological Bulletin, 76,* 128–148.

Fiedler, F. E. (1973). The contingency model—a reply to Ashour. *Organizational Behavior and Human Performance, 9,* 356–368.

Fiedler, F. E., & Chemers, M. (1974). *Leadership and effective management.* Glenview, IL: Scott Foresman.

Fiedler, F. E., Chemers, M. M. & Mahar, L. (1976). *Improving leadership effectiveness: The leader-match concept.* New York: Wiley.

Fiedler, F. E., & Leister, A. F. (1977). Leader intelligence and task performance: A test of a multiple screen model. *Organizational Behavior and Human Performance, 20,* 1–14.

Fiedler, F. E. & Mahar, L. (1979). The effectiveness of contingency model training: Validation of leader-match. *Personnel Psychology, 32,* 45–62.

Fiedler, F. E. & Meuwese, W. A. T. (1963). Leader's contribution to task performance in cohesive and uncohesive groups. *Journal of Abnormal and Social Psychology, 67,* 83–87.

Filley, A. C., House, R. J., & Kerr, S. (1976). *Managerial process and organizational behavior* (2nd ed.). Glenview, IL: Scott Foresman.

Firestone, I. J., Lichtman, C. M., & Colamosca, J. V. (1975). Leader effectiveness and leadership conferal as determinants of helping in a medical emergency. *Journal of Personality and Social Psychology, 31,* 243–248.

Fivars, G. (1973). *The critical incident technique: A bibliography.* Palo Alto, CA: American Institutes for Research.

Flanagan, J. C. (1954). The critical incident technique. *Psychological Bulletin, 51,* 327–358.

Fleishman, E. A. (1973). Twenty years of consideration and structure. In E. A. Fleishman & J. G. Hunt (Eds.), *Current developments in the study of leadership* (pp. 1–37). Carbondale, IL: Southern Illinois University Press.

Fleischman, E. A. & Harris, E. F. (1962). Patterns of leadership behavior related to employee grievance and turnover. *Personnel Psychology, 15,* 43–56.

Fleishman, E. A., & Simmons, J. (1970). Relationship between leadership patterns and effectiveness ratings among Israeli foremen. *Personnel Psychology, 23,* 169–172.

Frey, M. W. (1963). An experimental study of the influence of disruptive interaction induced by authoritarian–egalitarian, leader–follower combinations upon the decision-making effectiveness of small groups. *Dissertation Abstract, 25,* 897.

Friedan, B. (1981). *The second stage.* New York: Summit Books.

Fromkin, H. L. (1970). Effects of experimentally aroused feelings of undistinctiveness upon validation of scarce and novel experiences. *Journal of Personality and Social Psychology, 16,* 521–529.

Gamson, W. A., & Scotch, N. A. (1964). Scape-goating in baseball. *American Journal of Sociology, 70,* 69–72.

Garland, H., & Price, K. H. (1977). Attitudes toward women in management and attribution for their success and failure in a managerial position. *Journal of Applied Psychology, 62,* 29–33.

Gibb, C. (1969). Leadership. In G. Lindzey & E. Aronson (Eds.), *The handbook of social psychology* (Vol. 4, 2nd ed.). Reading, MA: Addison-Wesley.

Gilligan, C. (1982). *In a different voice.* Cambridge, MA: Harvard University Press.

Gintner, G., & Lindskold, S. (1975). Rate of participation and expertise as factors influencing leader choice. *Journal of Personality and Social Psychology, 32,* 1085–1089.

Ginzberg, E. (1966). *Life styles of educated women.* New York: Columbia University Press.

Glueck, W. F. (1980). *Management* (2nd ed.). New York: Holt, Rinehart, & Winston.

Goffman, E. (1959). *The presentation of self in everyday life.* Garden City, NY: Doubleday Anchor.

Goldman, M., & Fraas, L. A. (1965). The effects of leader selection on group performance. *Sociometry, 28,* 82–88.

Gouldner, A. W. (1960). The norm of reciprocity: A preliminary statement. *American Sociological Review, 25,* 161–178.

Graen, G. (1976). Role-making processes within complex organizations. In M. D. Dunnette (Ed.),

Handbook of industrial and organizational psychology, (pp. 1201–1245). Chicago, IL: Rand-McNally.

Graen, G., & Cashman, J. F. (1975). A role-making model of leadership in formal organizations: A developmental approach. In J. G. Hunt & L. C. Larson (Eds.), *Leadership frontiers*. Kent, OH: Comparative Administration Research Institute, Kent State University.

Graen, G., Dansereau, F., Minami, T. & Cashman, J. (1973). Leadership behaviors as cues to performance evaluation. *Academy of Management Journal, 16,* 611–623.

Graen, G., Orris, J. B., & Alvares, K. M. (1971). Contingency model of leadership effectiveness: Some experimental results. *Journal of Applied Psychology, 55,* 196–201.

Green, C. N. (1977). Disenchantment with leadership research: Some causes, recommendations, and alternative directions. In J. G. Hunt & L. L. Larson (Eds.), *Leadership: The cutting edge*. Carbondale, IL: Southern Illinois University Press.

Hackman, J. R., & Suttle, J. L. (1977). *Improving life at work*. Santa Monica, CA: Goodyear.

Hain, T. (1972). Determinants of changes in supervisory styles: an empirical test. *Proceedings of the Midwest Academy of Management.*

Hain, T., & Tabbs, S. (1974). Organizational development: The role of communication in diagnosis, change and evaluation. *Proceedings of the International Communication Association.*

Hall, J., & Donnell, S. M. (1979). Managerial achievement: The personal side of behavioral theory. *Human Relations, 32,* 77–101.

Halpin, A. W. (1954). The leadership behavior and combat performance of airplane commanders. *Journal of Abnormal and Social Psychology, 49,* 19–22.

Halpin, A. W. (1957a). *Manual for the leader behavior description questionnaire*. Columbus, OH: Ohio State University Bureau of Business Research.

Halpin, A. W. (1957b). The leader behavior and effectiveness of aircraft commanders. In R. M. Stogdill & A. E. Coons. (Eds.), *Leader behavior: Its description and measurement*. Columbus, OH: Ohio State University Bureau of Business Research.

Handbook of Labor Statistics: 1975 (reference ed.). (1975). Washington, DC: U.S. Dept. of Labor.

Hare, A. P. (1957). Situational differences in leader behavior. *Journal of Abnormal and Social Psychology, 55,* 132–135.

Hartman, D. P. (1977). Considerations in the choice of interobserver reliability estimates. *Journal of Applied Behavior Analysis, 10,* 103–116.

Haythorn, W. W., Couch, A., Haefner, D., Langham, P., & Carter, L. F. (1956). The effects of varying combinations of authoritarian and egalitarian leaders and followers. *Journal of Abnormal and Social Psychology, 53,* 210–219.

Hedrick, T. E., & Chance, J. E. (1977). Sex differences in assertive achievement patterns. *Sex Roles, 3,* 129–139.

Hemphill, J. K. (1954). A proposed theory of leadership in small groups: Second preliminary report. Columbus, OH: Ohio State University.

Hemphill, J. K., & Coons, A. E. (1957). Development of the leader behavior description questionnaire. In R. M. Stogdill & A. E. Coons (Eds.), *Leader behavior: Its description and measurement*. Columbus, OH: Bureau of Business Research, Ohio State University.

Hersey, P., & Blanchard, K. H. (1977). *Management of organizational behavior: Utilizing human resources* (3rd ed.). Englewood Cliffs, NJ: Prentice-Hall.

Hollander, E. P. (1964). *Leadership groups and influence*. New York: Oxford.

Hollander, E. P. (1958). Conformity, status, and idiosyncracy credit. *Psychological Review, 65,* 117–127.

Hollander, E. P. (1978). *Leadership dynamics: A practical guide to effective relationships*. New York: MacMillan Free Press.

Hollander, E. P. (1981). *Principles and methods of social psychology* (4th ed.). New York: Oxford.

Hollander, E. P., Fallon, B. J., & Edwards, M. T. (1977). Some aspects of influence and acceptability for appointed and elected leaders. *Journal of Psychology, 95,* 289–296.

Hollander, E. P., & Julian, J. W. (1969). Contemporary trends in the analysis of leadership processes. *Psychological Bulletin, 76,* 387–397.

Hollander, E. P., & Neider, L. L. (1977, July). *An exploratory study using critical incidents and rating scales to compare good and bad leadership* (Tech. Rep. No. 5). Buffalo, NY: State University of New York.

Hollander, E. P., & Yoder, J. D. (1980). Some issues comparing women and men as leaders. *Basic and Applied Social Psychology, 1,* 267–280.

Homans, G. C. (1950). *The human group.* New York: Harcourt Brace.

Homans, G. C. (1958). Social behavior as exchange. *American Journal of Sociology, 63,* 597–606.

Homans, G. C. (1961). *Social behavior: its elementary forms.* New York: Harcourt Brace.

Horner, M. S. (1970). Femininity and successful achievement: A basic inconsistency. In J. Bardwick, E. Douvan, M. S. Horner, & D. Gutmann, (Eds.), *Feminine psychology and conflict.* Monterey, CA: Brooks/Cole.

Horner, M. S. (1972). Toward an understanding of achievement-related conflicts in women. *Journal of Social Issues, 28,* 157–176.

House, R. J. (1968). Leadership training: Some dysfunctional consequences. *Administrative Science Quarterly, 12,* 556–571.

House, R. J., & Kerr, S. (1973). Organizational independence, leader behavior, and managerial practices: A replicated study. *Journal of Applied Psychology, 58,* 173–180.

Hunt, J. G., & Larson, L. L. (1977). *Leadership: The cutting edge.* Carbondale, IL: Southern Illinois University Press.

Hunt, J. G., & Osborne, R. N. (1982). Toward a macro-oriented model of leadership: An odyssey. In J. G. Hunt, U. Sekaran, & C. A. Schriesheim (Eds.), *Leadership: Beyond establishment views.* Carbondale, IL: Southern Illinois University Press.

Hunt, J. G., Sekaran, U., & Schriesheim, C. A. (1982). *Leadership: Beyond establishment views.* Carbondale, IL: Southern Illinois University Press.

Inderlied, S. D., & Powell, G. (1979). Sex-role identity and leadership style: Different labels for the same concept. *Sex Roles, 5,* 613–625.

Ivancevich, J. M., Szilagyi, A. D., & Wallace, M. J. (1977). *Organizational behavior and performance* (pp. 271–273). Santa Monica, CA: Goodyear.

Jacobs, T. O. (1971). *Leadership and exchange in formal organizations.* Alexandria, VA: Human Resources Research Organization.

Johnson, P. (1978). Women and power: Toward a theory of effectiveness. *Journal of Social Issues, 32,* 99–110.

Kanter, R. M. (1977). *Men and women of the corporation.* New York: Basic.

Kaplan, A. G., & Bean, J. P. (Eds.). (1976). *Beyond sex-role stereotypes: Readings toward a psychology of androgyny.* Boston, MA: Little Brown.

Katz, D., & Kahn, R. L. (1966). *The social psychology of organizations.* New York: Wiley.

Kelley, H. H. (1973). The process of causal attribution. *American Psychologist, 28,* 107–128.

Kerr, S., & Harlan, A. (1973). Predicting the effects of leadership training and experience from the contingency model: Some remaining problems. *Journal of Applied Psychology, 57,* 114–117.

Klauss, R., & Bass, B. M. (1981). *Impact of communication.* New York: Academic Press.

Kleinhans, B. & Taylor, D. A. (1976). Group processes, productivity, and leadership. In B. Seidenberg & A. Snadowsky (Eds.), *Social psychology.* New York: Macmillan.

Kline, B. E., & Martin, N. H. (1958). Freedom, authority, and decentralization. *Harvard Business Review, 36,* 69–75.

Koontz, H., O'Donnell, C., & Weihrich, H. (Eds.). (1980). *Management: a book of readings* (5th ed.). New York: McGraw Hill Inc.

Korman, A. K. (1966). "Consideration," "initiating structure," and organizational criteria. *Personnel Psychology, 18,* 349–360.

Korman, A. K. (1973). On the development of contingency theories of leadership: Some methodological considerations and possible alternatives. *Journal of Applied Psychology, 58,* 384–387.

Kuhn, T. (1962). *The structure of scientific revolutions.* Chicago, IL: University of Chicago Press.

Lakin, M. (1969). Some ethical issues in sensitivity training. *American Psychologists, 24,* 923–928.

Lamm, H. (1973). Intragroup effects on intergroup negotiations. *European Journal of Social Psychology, 3,* 179–192.

Landsberger, H. A. (1958). *Hawthorne revisited.* Ithaca, NY: Cornell University Press.

Lassey, W. R. (1976). Dimensions of leadership. In W. R. Lassey & R. R. Fernandez (Eds.), *Leadership and social exchange* (2nd ed.) (pp. 10–15). La Jolla, CA: University Associates.

Lawler, E. E. (1976). Control systems in organizations. In M. D. Dunnette (Ed.), *Handbook of industrial and organizational psychology* (pp. 1247–1290). Chicago, IL: Rand McNally.

Laws, J. L. (1975). The psychology of tokenism: an analysis. *Sex Roles, 1,* 51–67.

Lawshe, C. H., & Nagle, B. F. (1953). Productivity and attitude toward supervision. *Journal of Applied Psychology, 37,* 159–162.

Lewin, K., Lippit, R., & White, R. K. (1939). Patterns of aggressive behavior in experimentally created "social climates." *Journal of Social Psychology, 10,* 271–299.

Lieberson, S., & O'Connor, J. F. (1972). Leadership and organizational performance: A study of large corporations. *American Sociological Review, 37,* 117–130.

Likert, R. (1961). *New patterns of management.* New York: McGraw-Hill.

Likert, R. (1967). *The human organization.* New York: McGraw-Hill.

Llewellyn, C. (1981). Occupational mobility and the use of the comparative method. In H. Roberts (Ed.), *Doing feminist research.* Boston, MA: Rutledge & Kegan Paul.

Lord, R. G. (1977). Functional leadership behavior: Measurement and relation to social power and leadership perceptions. *Administrative Science Quarterly, 22,* 114–133.

Lowin, A., & Craig, J. R. (1968). The influence of level of performance on managerial style: an experimental object-lesson in the ambiguity of correlational data. *Organizational Behavior and Human Performance, 3,* 440–458.

Maccoby, E. E., & Jacklin, E. N. (1974). *The psychology of sex differences.* Stanford, CA: Stanford University Press.

Massengill, D., & DiMarco, N. (1979). Sex-role stereotypes and requisite management characteristics: a current replication. *Sex Roles, 5,* 561–570.

Mayo, E. (1953). *The human problems of an industrial organization.* New York: MacMillan.

McClelland, D. C. (1961). *The achieving society.* Princeton, NJ: Van Nostrand.

McGregor, D. (1960). *The human side of enterprise.* New York: McGraw-Hill.

Megargee, E. I. (1969). Influence of sex roles on the manifestation of leadership. *Journal of Applied Psychology, 53,* 377–382.

Merton, R. K. (1968). *Social theory and social structure* (2nd ed.). New York: Free Press.

Mischel, W. (1970). Sex-typing and socialization. In P. H. Mussen (Ed.), *Carmichael's manual of child psychology, II.* New York: Wiley.

Monahan, L., Kuhn, D., & Shaver, P. (1974). Intrapsychic versus cultural explanations of the "fear of success" motive. *Journal of Personality and Social Psychology, 29,* 60–64.

Moreno, J. L. (1955). *Sociodrama: A method for the analysis of social conflict.* Beacon, NY: Beacon House.

Morris, C. G. (1966). Task effects on group interaction. *Journal of Personality and Social Psychology, 4,* 545–554.

Morse, N. C. & Riemer, E. (1956). The experimental change of a major organizational variable. *Journal of Abnormal and Social Psychology, 52,* 120–129.

Morton, R. B., & Bass, B. M. (1964). The organizational training laboratory. *Training Directors Journal, 18,* 2–18.

National Organization of Women. (1981a). *ERA and employed women.* Washington, DC: author.

National Organization of Women. (1981b). *ERA and the 59¢ wage gap.* Washington, DC: author.

Neider, L. L., Carpenter, W. A., & Hollander, E. P. (1979, July). *Assessing good and bad leadership using critical incidents and ratings scales in three organizational settings: A follow-up study* (Tech. Rep. No. 8). Buffalo, NY: State University of New York.

Nord, W. R. (1977). Job Satisfaction reconsidered. *American Psychologist, 32,* 1026–1035.

Nutting, R. L. (1923). Some characteristics of leaders. *School and Society, 18,* 387–390.

O'Leary, V. E. (1974). Some attitudinal barriers to occupational aspirations in women. *Psychological Bulletin, 81,* 809–826.

Osborn, R. N., & Vicars, W. M. (1976). Sex stereotypes: An artifact in leader behavior and subordinate satisfaction analysis. *Academy of Management Journal, 19,* 439–449.

Oshry, B. I., & Harrison, R. (1966). Transfer from here-and-now to there-and-then: Changes in organizational problem diagnosis stemming from t-group training. *Journal of Applied Behavior Science, 2,* 185–198.

Pepinsky, P. N., Hemphill, J. K., & Shevitz, R. N. (1958). Attempts to lead, group productivity, and morale under conditions of acceptance and rejection. *Journal of Abnormal and Social Psychology, 57,* 47–54.

Pettigrew, T. (1961). Social psychology and desegregation research. *American Psychologist, 16,* 105–112.

Preston, M. G., & Heintz, R. K. (1949). Effects of participating vs. supervisory leadership on group judgment. *Journal of Abnormal and Social Psychology, 44,* 345–355.

Priest, R. F. (1975, June). *Improving prediction of fourth class leadership by reweighting components* (Tech. Rep. 75-019). West Point, NY: Office of Institution Research.

Priest, R. F., Grove, S., & Adams, J. (1980, September). *Historical and institutional perspectives on women in military academy roles.* Paper presented at the meetings of the American Psychological Association, Montreal, Quebec.

Ramirez, A. (1977). Chicano power and interracial group relations. In A. Ramirez (Ed.). *Chicano Psychology.* New York: Academic Press.

Raph, J. B., Goldberg, M. L., & Passow, A. H. (1966). *Bright underachievers: Studies of scholastic underachievement among intellectually superior high school students.* New York: Teachers College Press.

Raven, B. H., & French, J. R. P. (1958). Legitimate power, coercive power and observability in social influence. *Sociometry, 21,* 83–97.

Raven, B. H., & Kruglanski, A. W. (1970). Conflict and power. In P. Swingle (Ed.), *The structure of conflict.* New York: Academic Press.

Rice, R. W. (1976). The esteem for least preferred co-worker (LPC) score: What does it measure? *Dissertation Abstracts International, 36.*

Rice, R. W. (1978a). Psychometric properties of the esteem for least preferred co-worker (LPC) scale. *Academy of Management Review, 3,* 106–118.

Rice, R. W. (1978b). Construct validity of the least preferred co-worker score. *Psychological Bulletin, 85,* 1199–1237.

Rice, R. W. (1979). Reliability and validity of the lpc scale: A reply. *Academy of Management Review, 4,* 291–294.

Rice, R. W., Bender, L. R., & Vitters, A. G. (1980). Leader sex, follower attitudes toward women and leadership effectiveness: A laboratory experiment. *Organizational Behavior and Human Performance, 25,* 46–78.

Rice, R. W., Bender, L. R., & Vitters, A. G. (1982). *Validity tests of the contingency model for female and male leaders.* Unpublished manuscript.

Rice, R. W., Instone, D., & Adams, J. (1981, August). *The 1979 leadership study: Correlates of leadership success for male and female leaders.* Paper presented at the Academy of Management National Convention, San Diego, CA.

Rice, R. W., Instone, D., & Adams, J. (1984). Leader sex, leader success, and leadership process: Two field studies. *Journal of Applied Psychology, 69,* 12–31.

Rice, R. W., Yoder, J. D., Adams, J., Priest, R. F., & Prince, H. T. (1984). Leadership ratings for male and female military cadets. *Sex Roles, 10,* 885–902.

Riger, S., & Galligan, P. (1980). Women in management: An exploration of competing paradigms. *American Psychologist, 35,* 902–910.

Robertson, I. (1977). *Sociology,* New York: Warth.

Rossi, A. S. (1976). Sex equality: The beginnings of ideology. In A. G. Kaplan & J. P. Bean (Eds.), *Beyond sex-role stereotypes: Readings toward a psychology of androgyny.* Boston, MA: Little Brown.

Rothlisberger, F. J., & Dickson, W. J. (1939). *Management and the worker.* Cambridge, MA: Harvard University Press.

Rotter, J. B. (1966). Generalized expectancies for internal and external control of reinforcement. *Psychological Monographs, 80,* Whole No. 609, 1–28.

Ryan, W. (1976). *Blaming the victim* (rev. ed.). New York: Vintage.

Salanick, G. R., & Pfeffer, J. (1977). Constraints on administrator discretion: The limited influence of mayors on city budgets. *Urban Affairs Quarterly, 12,* 475–496.

Sayles, L. R. (1964). *Managerial behavior: Administration in complex organization.* New York: McGraw-Hill.

Schein, V. E. (1973). The relationship between sex role stereotypes and requisite management characteristics. *Journal of Applied Psychology, 57,* 95–100.

Schriesheim, C. A. (1977). Theories and measures of leadership, critical appraisal of current and future directions. In J. G. Hunt & L. L. Larson (Eds.), *Leadership: the cutting edge* (pp. 9–20). Carbondale, IL: Southern Illinois University Press.

Schriesheim, C. A., House, R. J., & Kerr, S. (1976). Leader initiating structure: A reconciliation of discrepant research results and some empirical tests. *Organizational Behavior and Human Performance, 15,* 297–321.

Schriesheim, C. A., & Kerr, S. (1974). Psychometric properties of the Ohio State leadership scales. *Psychological Bulletin, 81,* 756–765.

Scott, E. L. (1952). *Perceptions of organization and leadership behavior.* Columbus, OH: Ohio State University Research Foundation.

Shartle, C. L. (1950). Studies of leadership by interdisciplinary methods. In A. G. Grace (Ed.), *Leadership in American education.* Chicago, IL: University of Chicago Press.

Shaw, M. C., & McCuen, J. T. (1960). The onset of academic underachievement in bright children. *Journal of Educational Psychology, 51,* 103–108.

Shaw, M. E. (1955). A comparison of two types of leadership in various communication nets. *Journal of Abnormal and Social Psychology, 50,* 127–134.

Sherif, M., & Sherif, C. W. (1956). *An outline of social psychology.* New York: Harper.

Skinner, B. F. (1974). *About Behaviorism.* New York: Knopf.

Sorrentino, R. M., & Boutillier, R. G. (1975). The effect of quantity and quality of verbal interaction on ratings of leadership ability. *Journal of Experimental Social Psychology, 11,* 403–411.

Spence, J. T., & Helmreich, R. (1972). The attitudes toward women scale: An objective instrument to measure attitudes toward rights and roles of women in contemporary society. *Journal Supplement Abstract Service, 2,* 66.

Spence, J. T., & Helmreich, R. L. (1978). *Masculinity and femininity their psychological dimensions, correlates, and antecedents.* Austin, TX: University of Texas Press.

Spence, J. T., Helmreich, R. L., & Stapp, J. (1973). A short version of the attitude toward women scale (aws). *Bulletin of Psychonomic Society, 2,* 219–20.

Spence, J. T., Helmreich, R., & Stapp, J. (1974). The personal attributes questionnaire: A measure of sex-role, stereotypes, and masculinity-femininity. *Journal Supplement Abstract Service, 4,* 43.

Stein, A. H., & Bailey, M. M. (1973). The socialization of achievement orientation in females. *Psychological Bulletin, 80,* 345–366.

Stiehm, J. H. (1981). *Bring me men and women: Mandated change at the U.S. Air Force Academy.* Berkeley, CA: University of California Press.

Stogdill, R. M. (1948). Personal factors associated with leadership: A survey of the literature. *Journal of Psychology, 25,* 35–71.

Stogdill, R. M. (1974). *Handbook of Leadership.* New York: Free Press.

Stogdill, R. M. (1977). *Leadership abstracts and bibliography, 1970–1974.* Columbus, OH: College of Administrative Sciences #AA-10.

Stogdill, R. M. (1980). Historical trends in leadership theory and research. In H. Koontz, C. O'Donnell, & H. Weihrich (Eds.). *Management: A book of readings,* (5th ed.) (pp. 524–532). New York: McGraw-Hill.

Stogdill, R. M., Shartle, C. L., Scott, E. L., Coons, A. E., & Jaynes, W. E. (1956). *A predictive study of administrative work patterns.* Columbus, OH: Ohio State University, Bureau of Business Research.

Szilagyi, A. D., & Wallace, M. J. (1980). *Organizational behavior and performance* (2nd ed.). Santa Monica, CA: Goodyear.

Szilagyi, A. D. (1979). Reward behavior of male and female leaders: A causal inference analysis. *Journal of Vocational Behavior, 16,* 59–72.

Thibaut, J. W., & Kelley, H. H. (1959). *The social psychology of groups.* New York: Wiley.

Thibaut, J. W., & Riecken, H. W. (1955). Some determinants and consequences of the perception of social causality. *Journal of Personality, 24,* 113–133.

Tosi, H. J. (1982). Toward a paradigm shift in the study of leadership. In J. G. Hunt, U. Sekaran, & C. A. Schriesheim, (Eds.), *Leadership: Beyond establishment views.* Carbondale, IL: Southern Illinois University Press.

Touhey, J. C. (1974). Effects of additional women professionals on ratings of occupational prestige and desirability. *Journal of Personality and Social Psychology, 29,* 86–89.

Tuckman, B. W. (1965). Developmental sequence in small groups. *Psychological Bulletin, 63,* 384–399.

Unger, R. K. (1979). Toward a redefinition of sex and gender, *American Psychologist, 34,* 1085–1094.

U.S. Bureau of the Census. (1981). *Statistical Abstracts of the United States: 1981* (102nd ed.) (1981). Washington, DC: Author.

Vitters, A. G. (1978, June). *Report of the admission of women to the U.S. Military Academy, Project Athena, II.* West Point, NY: U.S. Military Academy.

Vitters, A. G., & Kinzer, N. S. (1977, September). *Report of admission of women to the U.S. Military Academy, Project Athena.* West Point, NY: U.S. Military Academy.

Vroom, V. H. (1976). Leadership. In M. D. Dunnette, (Ed.), *Handbook of industrial and organizational psychology* (pp. 1527, 1536–1548). Chicago, IL: Rand McNally.

Walker, C. R., & Guest, R. H. (1952). *The man of the assembly line.* Cambridge, MA: Harvard University Press.

Weber, M. (1947). *The theory of social and economic organization.* New York: Free Press.

Wertheimer, J. (1972). *Fundamental issues in psychology.* New York: Holt.

West, N. (1976). *Leadership With a Feminine Cast.* San Francisco, CA: R and F Research Associates.

Women increase their numbers in Congress. (1980). *Congressional Quarterly Weekly Report, 38*(45), p. 3303.

Yoder, J. D. (1983, March). *Queen bees or tokens?: Person-versus situation-centered approaches to mentors.* Paper presented at the meetings of the Association for Women in Psychology, Seattle, WA.

Yoder, J. D. (1983). Another look at women in the United States Army: a comment on Woelfel's article. *Sex Roles, 9,* 285–288.

Yoder, J. D., & Adams, J. (1984). Women entering non traditional roles: When work demands and sex-roles conflict. *International Journal of Women's Studies, 7,* 260–272.

Yoder, J. D., Adams, J., Grove, S. & Priest, R. F. (1984). To teach is to learn: reducing tokenism with mentors. *Psychology of Women Quarterly 9*(1).

Yoder, J. D., Adams, J., & Prince, H. T. (1983). The price of a token. *Journal of Political and Military Sociology, 11,* 325–337.

Yoder, J. D., Rice, R. W., & Adams, J. (1979, June). *Tests of Fiedler's screen model of leadership* (Tech. Rep. 394). Washington DC: U.S. Army Research Institute for the Behavioral and Social and Behavioral Sciences.

Yoder, J. D., Rice, R. W., Adams, J., Priest, R. F., & Prince, H. T. (1982). Reliability of the attitudes toward women scale (AWS) and personal attributes questionnaire (PAQ). *Sex Roles, 8,* 651–657.

Yoder, J. D., Rice, R. W., Adams, J., Prince, H. T., & Hicks, J. M. (1979). *The relationship between leader personality characteristics and group task performance.* (Technical Report). Washington, DC: U.S. Army Research Institute for the Social & Behavioral Sciences.

Yoder, J. D., & Sinnett, L. M. (in press). Is it all in a number? a case study of tokenism. *Psychology of Women Quarterly.*

Zdep, S. M., & Oakes, W. I. (1967). Reinforcement of leadership behavior in group discussion. *Journal of Experimental Social Psychology, 3,* 310–320.

Author Index

Italics indicate bibliographic citations.

Subject Index